GAME ON THE GRILL

THE ART OF BARBECUING, GRILLING, AND SMOKING WILD GAME

By Eileen Clarke

Voyageur Press

Edited by Gretchen Bratvold
Designed by Kjerstin Moody
Printed in Hong Kong

01   02   03   04   05   5   4   3   2   1

Library of Congress Cataloging-in-Publication Data
Clarke, Eileen.
    Game on the grill : the art of barbecuing, grilling, and smoking wild game / by Eileen Clarke.
    p. cm.– (The fish and game kitchen)
    ISBN 0-89658-344-9
    1. Cookery (Game) 2. Barbecue cookery. I. Title. II. Series.

TX751 .C582 2001
641.6'91–dc21

                                                                        00-043797

Distributed in Canada by Raincoast Books, 9050 Shaughnessy Street, Vancouver, B.C. V6P 6E5

Published by Voyageur Press, Inc.
123 North Second Street, P.O. Box 338, Stillwater, MN 55082 U.S.A.
651-430-2210, fax 651-430-2211
books@voyageurpress.com
www.voyageurpress.com

Educators, fundraisers, premium and gift buyers, publicists, and marketing managers:
Looking for creative products and new sales ideas? Voyageur Press books are available at special discounts when purchased in quantities, and special editions can be created to your specifications. For details contact the marketing department at 800-888-9653.

Page 1: *Bonneville Tenderloin*

CONTENTS

Creamed Pheasant with Caramelized Onions

Wild Turkey and Sage Sausage (patties), Pheasant and Apple Sausage (links)

INTRODUCTION

I remember the barbecue. My father would put on his one pair of Saturday blue jeans and douse a whole bag of charcoal briquettes with lighter fluid in our uncovered, spindly legged, upside down Frisbee of a barbecue and, with a great flurry, grill two steaks. Very quickly. Then he'd call for my mother to bring a platter, and he'd waltz those steaks into the house while the coals continued to burn, unused, for the next hour. Perhaps your father was into true barbecuing, long-cooking briskets and hams as it has been done for generations in those great bastions of true barbecue, Kansas City, the Carolinas, and Texas.

Well, times and barbecues have changed. From those inverted Frisbees of the fifties, we developed the hibachi of the sixties, the little aluminum smoking boxes of the seventies, the covered kettle grill of the eighties, and the affordable propane unit of the nineties. My father's little summer cooker has become a year-round outdoor grill, ready at the turn of a valve. But what about those true barbecuers? Has technology forgotten them? Not hardly. The latest piece of equipment to show up on the back porch is the water smoker, and while it is not yet as popular as the propane grill, it may soon become the first pit-smoking substitute.

Are baby boomers guilty once again of transforming the face of America? Who knows. All I know is that barbecuing and grilling is getting easier to do. No longer do you have to wait for a warm summer day or thirty minutes to see if the coals have really started. You don't even have to have a backyard or the patience of Job. And with that, it is about time we challenged the traditional ideas about what we barbecue and grill. Namely, it doesn't have to be fatty beef, pork, and chicken anymore. It doesn't even have to be tender. And it doesn't have to take days.

This book opens up a world of cooking to people who have a freezer full of game meat—anything and everything from tender steaks to tough briskets, and succulent goose to tough old rooster legs. Using the three most popular tools for barbecuing—charcoal grills, propane grills, and Little Chief smokers—plus that new boy on the block, the water smoker, we will transform what tradition tells us is not fat or tender enough for anything but the stew pot. From hot-grilling elk steaks, to roasting half-frozen whitetail rumps, to moist-smoking spicy goose sausage, and slow-smoking venison salami, we will do it all. We'll even learn a few tricks about marinades, wood, and how to prolong the life of your charcoal fire, as well as tips to slow down that hot-blooded propane grill. So thaw a chunk of this year's bird, last year's rutty buck, or that brisket that's been rolling around the freezer since you graduated from high school and let's get cooking.

Elsie delivers a fine rooster pheasant to her hunting partner.

STEP BY STEP

Top Ten Myths and Legends of Game Care

Often, the myths we live by have a grain of truth. More often, they had a grain of truth in a particular situation or place that either we never lived in or that doesn't exist anymore. We end up with this list of things we think we have to do that, in fact, do not apply to our environment or our times. Beginning with that old bugaboo, the tarsal gland, and including the great American debate over how charred that steak should be, here's the truth behind a few of the more popular stories.

• *"If you don't remove the tarsal gland your meat will taste musky."*

Here's a perfect example of a partial truth. The truth is that the tarsal gland, located on the lower leg in different places according to species, is only one source of musk. When deer, elk, and other ungulates rut in the fall, the tarsal gland secretes musk that the male uses to attract females. There are three other glands that do the same thing, but hunters have never blamed those glands for bad taste. The tarsal gland is unique in only one other very important way: Male deer urinate on it during the rut.

As a general rule, however, humans don't eat the lower legs of ungulates. Tarsal glands are not located where they will come in contact with the meat unless we initiate that contact ourselves. Leave them alone and they will not taint the meat. Cut them off as the first step of field dressing, and you stand a good chance of tracking both musk and urine straight onto the meat.

I have never cut out the tarsal glands. This not only reduces the chance of contaminating the meat, but also cuts down the amount of work I have to do in the field. If you must cut them off, do it last, after you are completely done handling the meat. Then, before you use that knife again, wash it in hot, soapy water. Musk is an oil; urine is full of impurities: Merely wiping or rinsing the blade in snow or clean water is not enough.

And while you're at it, wear rubber gloves when handling freshly killed animals. Recently, a Montana man contracted brucellosis in the course of his work. The work? He collected urine from elk and deer to be processed into aromatic hunting baits. The Montana state veterinarian says that since brucellosis is mainly a reproductive system disease, hunters face little danger of catching it when they field dress game animals. But he does recommend rubber gloves whenever people handle wild animals.

• *"There is only one way to field dress a deer. My way."*

There are three basic methods for transporting meat from the field. The first avoids field dressing entirely and simply bones the meat from the outside of the carcass. The other two methods are more common and include the method I usually use: to split the pelvis and draw the digestive tract through the split, intact. The third method leaves the pelvis intact, instead tying off the anus, and cutting it free of the surrounding tissue to draw it back through the pelvis. I have seen people argue loudly and write long and arrogantly about which is the right way. Personally, I'd rather argue over how many grains of powder will produce the highest velocity in a 130-grain bullet. Which is to say, there is a point at which argument is simply argument.

The one and true purpose of field dressing is to separate the delicious meat of your trophy animal from its last meal without having one touch the other. Any method that cleanly removes the meat from the skeleton, or the offal from the carcass, and is something you are comfortable with and doesn't take an inordinate amount of time, is the best method. Having said that, I

A perfect day for hunting Canada geese. (Photograph © John Barsness)

will point out that my husband, John, can field dress a deer-sized animal in less than three minutes using the split pelvis method. It takes me fifteen, but, having watched him do it for the better part of two decades, I am convinced I'd be slower at any method I used. Do we do it the right way? I don't hear any complaints at the table.

• *"Never let water touch the meat or it will spoil."* I read this one about three years ago in one of the most popular sporting magazines in the business. Water is bad, the alleged expert said. Well, no. Water is just water, unless you are hunting in Alaska where it rains constantly, the rivers are full of dying and decaying salmon, and, often, you have to pack the animal out a minimum of one to two days before it is safely deposited in a clean, dry place. Yes, rinsing an animal in carrion-laden water (which most probably has a high bacterial content), and constant immersion in water, no matter how clean it appears, is not good.

But most of us don't live where the annual precipitation is more than two hundred inches (5 m) a year and where fish spawn and die in such copious numbers that they pollute the clean water for miles around. According to surveys conducted every few years by major outdoor magazines, most of us hunt less than one hundred miles (161 km) from home. Nine times out of ten, the deer, elk, antelope, or moose is safely home, under shelter, before any rain falls on it.

Let's look at the usual circumstance: You go out hunting and the ground is dry, and composed of dirt and dead leaves. In the process of field dressing, a small amount of dirt, plus the animal's own hair and blood can get on the meat. In most areas, snow is a factor during hunting season, and, while a deep, cold snow almost eliminates all the dirt, a small amount of melting snow gets everything muddy. Wet dirt is always harder to control than dry dirt, and blood and hair are endemic. Left on, all three will make the meat gamy tasting. Rinsing the inside of the body cavity and any exposed meat with clean water—either from your garden hose, a clean creek, or a pile of fresh snow—is the easiest and most efficient way to remove contaminants.

I hunt whitetail not far from my house. I drive five

Closing out the pheasant season.

minutes up the creek from my house, hop a fence, walk across an alfalfa field, and cross the creek. If I'm lucky, in a few hours I come back across the creek with a white-tail deer in tow. Now whitetails, traditionally, don't co-operate much in this towing part of the hunt, and I have found the easiest way to go from point A to point B—where my truck is parked—is to float the deer down the twists and turns of the creek until it bends pretty close to the road. That drag only takes about ten min-utes, and, by the time I pull the deer out of the creek, any remnant of blood and hair has been swept clean. In another ten minutes, it's hanging in my barn drip-drying. My home creek deer have always been delicious.

Do not be afraid to use a clean water or clean snow rinse to wipe away contaminants. Once in the field and once again at home is usually good enough. You want the meat to be free of the gamy flavors contaminants cause. Do not, however, let the carcass sit in the water or the water sit in the carcass for more than a few min-utes. And use only clean, cold water. There's a reason the Alaska effect gets written up.

• *"Freezing a whole carcass ruins the meat."*
Followed closely by: "You have to butcher and
freeze the animal immediately, or it will sour."
It's the age-old question: How do we get the best tast-ing, most tender meat? The biology is this: The deer, moose, elk, caribou, etc., while alive, has a temperature of around 104° F (40° C). Optimum aging temperature is 35° to 45° F (2° to 7° C), and with very careful tending as high as 55° F (13° C). To have tender, good-tasting meat the animal needs to go from 104° to 55° F (40° to 13° C) within the first twelve hours after the kill, and it must start that journey within the first four hours. In that twelve hours, the animal goes from being warm and pliable to very hard—rigor mortis setting in—and back again to being somewhat pliable—rigor mortis coming out—and cool. That's all happening in that same approximate half-day, faster or slower depending on ambient air temperature. What hasn't been happening yet is aging.

Which gets us back to the first half of the cold myth: Freezing a whole carcass ruins the meat. The statement is half true: Freezing the carcass—or any part of the meat—during rigor mortis will make the meat very tough, whether it froze naturally outdoors, or in your freezer. After the fact, no amount of aging, stewing, or pot roasting will improve it. On the other hand, if you let the carcass hang too long or too warm, it will sour.

Glassing the prairie for antelope. (Photograph © John Barsness)

HOW TOUGH IS YOUR DEER, ELK, MOOSE? TEST A SHOULDER STEAK

Whether you age your meat or not, it's still a good idea to test the animal for tenderness and flavor before you cut it up. That takes the guesswork out of cooking wild game meat. Here's the easiest and most reliable way I've found.

As soon as possible, cut a small chunk of meat (about 2–3 inches/5–7½ cm square and 1 inch/2½ cm thick) from the shoulder (see drawing). Weather permitting, toss it on the grill over high heat and cook it about 2–3 minutes a side. Indoors, melt 2 tablespoons of butter in a skillet, increase the heat to high, then fry the steak about 3–4 minutes a side. Then slice it.

If you can slice the steak with a fork, you're way ahead of the game; with a table knife, still doing very well. If you need a paring or boning knife, it signals trouble. Since the shoulder is the tougher part of any animal, a tender shoulder steak is a sign that the whole animal will be quite easy to handle. A really tough shoulder steak usually means the whole animal will be tough. Somewhere in between really tough and easy-to-slice can give you a mixture of tender rear quarters with tough front quarters.

Perfect aging weather is between 35° and 45° F (1°–7° C), in a clean, bug-free place. At that temperature, do the shoulder test again every 3–4 days. Usually in 7–10 days there's a noticeable improvement in texture. At 2 weeks—only at the lowest range of aging temperature—tenderness will reach its peak. If the animal isn't tender now, it will never be tender. But, before you start grinding the shoulder meat, do a taste test on the rump (in the area corresponding to the shoulder test location). If the hindquarter is tough as well, just throw that into the grinder, too. And remember, there's no tragedy in eating baked ziti and brats.

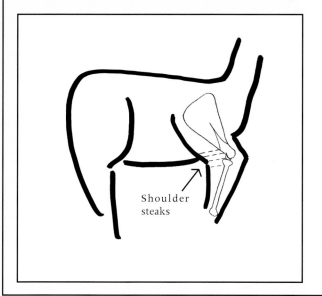

To cut a test steak, slice across the grain at the shoulder as shown.

Shoulder steaks

Great tasting venison at the table begins with proper field dressing and cooling down the animal in the first four hours. (Photograph © John Barsness)

WHEN IS IT DONE AGING?

At 35°–45° F (1°–7° C), you can safely age an animal for 10–14 days. Just be sure you have it in a clean, bug-free environment, and do the shoulder test 2–3 times over the course of aging. Your animal may not need 2 weeks.

To tell when you've reached the limit of safety: Over the course of the aging, the outer, exposed edges of meat will form a dark, dry crust. This is okay. Some epicures even prefer the dark, dry crust. But you need to stop the aging process and butcher the meat at the first sign of mold. I know people who let meat age past the first sign of mold. It's risky, unless you know what you're doing and don't have any distractions in your life.

At higher temperatures, say 50°–60° F (10°–16° C), this whole process gallops along, and unless you feel confident with aging, have done it before, and work at home so you can check three times a day, you're best off just processing your animal within 8 hours after rigor mortis comes out. Look for the knees and neck to bend again, almost as easily as when you field dressed the animal.

Here's what I do and recommend to beginners: If mold appears, and it will first appear as tiny circles of white and pale green fuzz, trim it off. Then process the animal immediately. Place the packages in the freezer so that the cold air can reach all around and the meat freezes solid in 24 hours. That's what stops the aging. At 0 to -5° F (-18 to -15° C) you can properly freeze 1 ½ pounds (¾ kg) of loosely stacked packages of meat per 1 square foot (78 square cm) of freezer space.

The happy medium, what is best for good taste and texture, is to cool the meat down to 55° to 35° F (13° to 2° C) in twelve hours, then hang it to age in a bug-free enclosure for anywhere from two to seven days at 35° to 55° F (2° to 13° C)—less time at warmer temperatures, more time at cooler ones—then butcher and freeze. With the exception of antelope and young-of-the-year, the process of aging will tenderize all animals. One-and-a-half-year-old animals should be tender with two days in any temperature above freezing. But every animal will gain a better and more complex flavor with a little aging. Even whitetail does.

What happens in practice? Here's a tale of three animals. My friend Tom McIntyre went on a trip to Anticosti Island, Quebec, and shot a three-and-a-half-year-old whitetail buck on a Tuesday, in mild weather. He skinned and quartered the deer and packed it into a cooler. On the way home, the airline lost the deer. The buck had hung two days at the lodge, traveled two days with Tom, then traveled three days more on his own. Tom was concerned, since the deer had not been frozen before leaving Anticosti, but it aged nicely in those seven days, traveling in the cold belly of airplanes and sitting in poorly heated hangars.

The second deer was mine, a two-and-a-half-year-old mule deer buck shot on a cool October day in eastern Montana. I field dressed it and stretched it across the roof of my topper, then headed home. It had cooled down nicely by the time I got home, and we hung it in the barn to age. Problem was two days later the thermometer plummeted and the deer froze. Since I'm allergic to the fur, we couldn't bring it inside to thaw, and so it hung in the barn, frozen. Every time it warmed up a bit, we'd go outside and knock on his rib cage, but it was a consistently cold winter, and he didn't thaw till March. At least three people told us he'd be dry and stringy—or rotten—but he wasn't, though he never aged any more than those first two days. When he thawed, we butchered him up right away, afraid he'd freeze again, and we'd have to spend our entire spring knocking on his ribcage. The meat was as delicious and tender as any animal we've ever cooked. He froze after rigor mortis had gone out, so he was tender, and leaving his skin on kept the meat moist.

The third animal was a five-and-a-half-year-old elk. He hit the ground Saturday night, and the guys butchered him up Sunday morning, twelve short hours later. The elation at safely putting a bull in the freezer paled in the next few months. First, it was cold the night the elk was killed, and rigor mortis had not come out before they started butchering and freezing the meat. That made him tough. Second, that Saturday night was October 26: That's the end of the rut around here, and that bull hadn't had enough time to gain back the weight he had lost running around chasing cows and not eating right. That made him gamy. And third? It was a mature animal, and it wasn't aged a whit. A spike elk may not need aging to be tender, but a mature bull will benefit greatly. I've heard a lot about that elk over the last few years. None of it good.

• *"Skin taints the meat."*
Depending on where you live and when you hunt, this myth has more truth that most. If you hunt in hot weather, leaving the skin on will keep the carcass from cooling down as quickly as it needs to. Not cooling down the meat within twelve hours of the kill (and *starting* to cool it within four hours) will definitely flavor your meat unfavorably. I usually hunt in cool weather, or at least on days when nights are pretty cool. If you're hunting in shirt sleeves weather, and shoot something early in the day, you would do well to skin the carcass after field dressing. If it will be evening—and the nights are 50° F (10° C) or cooler—within four hours of killing the animal, don't skin it. Leaving the skin on will keep the carcass clean, thus avoiding another cause of tainting.

One of the reasons I split the pelvis when field dressing is to allow air to thoroughly circulate between and around the hind quarters, so it cools down faster. I also split the sternum. You can run your knife—or saw, for larger animals—up one side of the sternum, where the ribs attach, and cut through the ligaments that hold them on. This allows air to circulate through the front quarters. The front quarters will sour first, so if it's warm, I'll go a step further and remove the head at the base of the neck and the esophagus. All this can be done to help cool the carcass faster without having to resort to skinning. (If you do remove the head, double-check your tag to see if you must leave the milk sack or penis sheath attached to the carcass for proof of sex.)

So how can you be sure you've done enough? Feel the meat. If it still feels equal to your own body temperature after a couple of hours, you need to take more steps to help cool it down. Often, when it's warm enough to skin the carcass, you really also need to quarter it and hang it in the shade, or over a stream to allow more cool air to get to it. If you're close to civilization, you can get a block or two of ice to place in the chest cavity.

A classic side by side and a classic bird. (Photograph © Doug Stamm/ProPhoto)

We also freeze water in plastic pop bottles to insert in smaller spaces. (The space for the esophagus is a good candidate.)

If your animal was young and healthy, and you have done everything possible to cool and clean the carcass, and you still have gamy meat, check with your local game department. Sometimes the available feed will affect the taste of animals. My friend Melvin Forbes of West Virginia tells me that when the white-oak acorn crop fails and the deer eat red-oak acorns all fall, they develop a bitter flavor. He has found that skinning the deer immediately will prevent the flavor from being transferred to the meat. Soybeans can also affect the meat, making it dark-colored and livery tasting.

Rutting mule deer, elk, and caribou, and any animal that has been losing weight, either from the rut or some injury or illness, are bound to be gamy. It will help the cook to ruthlessly trim fat, sinew, and connective tissue from these animals, since gamy flavors most often are stored there. Other than that, I have found that the main cause of tainted meat is some failure in game care, not the skin itself.

• *"Wild meat has to be marinated to taste good."*
A man called me up after a terrible game dinner. "A friend gave me this piece of venison and told me to marinate the hell out of it, then cook it. So I marinated it in white wine and it was terrible."

The first rule of cooking is red wine with red meat, and white wine with white meat. But the first rule of giving hard-won game meat away is to keep the prime stuff to yourself. So my first instinct is not to blame the marinade. I wish I'd asked the caller if he even liked game meat.

Having said that, I'll admit that I don't marinate much myself. It takes time and energy, and since I'm pretty much a meat hunter rather than a trophy hunter, I like the taste of the meat in my freezer. My husband, however, likes to hunt big mule deer. Most years he eats his tag. Then he'll get lucky, and some of those deer will take a lot of trimming, marinating, and creative sausage recipes. But as soon as someone tells me that all game meat has to be marinated, I'm suspicious—both of the meat and the cook.

Not all venison needs to be marinated to taste good. If your game meat has been kept clean of hair, blood, and dirt and has been aged properly, trimmed of dried and bloodshot meat as well as most of the fat, sinew, and connective tissue, then butchered with care, you should not have to marinate it to be edible. (The exceptions are the aforementioned rutting mule deer, caribou, elk, and musk ox, or any animal that has lost weight from illness or injury. They're not always gamy but are your usual suspects. In my many years of cooking game meats, I've found that whitetail and antelope bucks are not as universally plagued by the rut.) I use marinades as a treat. And they don't have to be fancy or complicated to add variety to your freezer fare.

There are lots of things you can use for marinades. The point of the marinade is to add moisture, tenderness, and flavor: with a little oil, acid, and spice, respectively. The oil can be anything you have on hand. I use a lot of canola because it has a high smoking point, it's locally grown, and it's said to reduce the risk of coronary heart disease. The acid can be wine, hard liquor, citrus juice, or flavored vinegars. One of the best meals I've had recently was a grilled pheasant breast that had been marinated for forty-eight hours in oil, raspberry vinegar, and poppy seeds. I regularly make a winter casserole with shoulder steaks marinated in orange and lime juice. The spice can be anything you're hungry for—complex and exotic, fiery hot, or mildly tingly. Or just a little salt and pepper.

Waterfowl, with their darker meat and robust flavors, should be treated, for the most part, like red meat. Some animals, such as sharp-tail grouse and late season diving ducks, will probably always need help. But if you have to marinate every chunk of wild meat in your freezer, you have three choices: rethink your game care, give up trophy hunting, or get creative with marinades.

• *"Always cook your game meat very well done to kill all the bugs."*
I propose that this notion came from a time when market hunting was still rampant and health departments nonexistent. Tainted food, not just game, was a life-threatening problem until the widespread use of chemical preservatives, freezers, and refrigerators. Food poisoning and botulism are serious business. Don't take chances. All meats are perishable. But hunters have an advantage over shoppers. We can control the care of game meat from the shot to the table.

While you are field dressing the deer, look the animal over: check the liver for flukes, the muscle for parasites—all very obvious things. Healthy red meat is not only red, but also smooth with no spots, bumps, or other colored shapes. Whenever possible, don't take animals that look unhealthy on the hoof. An animal that is los-

A bugling bull elk. (Photograph © John Barsness)

ing weight may not have any diseases or parasites, but the meat simply won't be prime. So check them over, before and after the shot. Avoid the skinny, the dull-eyed, the less-than-perfect-looking hides. And if you have doubts, have your local veterinarian take a look after the shot. In some states, including Montana, if a veterinarian certifies that an animal is not fit for consumption, the fish and game department will issue you another tag. But remember also that Mother Nature is not a gentle mother. If an animal is sick, there's little chance it will outrun the four-legged predators very long.

In other words, if it gets as far as your freezer, there is no more reason to char game meat than to overcook beef or chicken. If anything, game meat's lower fat content means you must be especially careful not to overcook. The fat in commercial meat makes it much more forgiving, as well as more unhealthy as a steady diet.

For best results with venison, follow the recommendation on a standard meat thermometer for rare, medium rare, or just medium, and remember that any roast or whole bird will rise 10° F (6° C) after it's out of the oven. Birds, if raised in the wild, can be cooked rare. Pen-raised birds, however, if released for hunting, should be cooked to the 170° F (77° C) recommended for all poultry. Close quarters are always a breeding ground for disease, and you need to cook the birds well to avoid worry.

If you don't have a meat thermometer, you can test pale-meated birds (such as blue grouse or pheasant) by piercing the breast with the point of a knife: if rare, the juices run red; if medium, it runs pink; and if well done, clear. We cook all commercial birds until the juice runs clear because they are pen raised. Healthy wild birds can be cooked rare and are much juicier that way.

Red meat can be finger-tested: press the steak. Rare meat will feel soft; well done, hard. This is an age-old method, but it may take some practice. If in doubt, simply slice one piece off the end of the steak or roast. Generally the end will be one stage more cooked than the center; so bright pink on the end means raw red in the middle. Cooked rare to medium, venison is moist and tender; cook it well done, and it can be dry and tough, just like overcooked beef.

• *"Always parboil wild birds, to remove excess fat before cooking."*

Depending on the cookbook, I've seen this recommendation for everything from waterfowl to ruffed and blue grouse. The cooks who write those lines year after year are cooking domestically raised "wild" birds. They're the ones with all the fat. They don't migrate, or forage, or get foraged upon. If you don't believe me, check out the "wild" mallards that hang out at the Jack Daniel's Distillery in Lynchberg, Tennessee. If you look up the word "waddle" in the dictionary, there's a picture of Jack's Ducks. Like commercially fed waterfowl, they're fed a diet of barley, rice, wheat, and corn, designed to fatten them for the table. If every mallard in my freezer ate that well, I'd have to parboil them, too.

The problem has always been, especially with upland birds, how to keep them moist while cooking. Thus the abundance of quail wrapped in bacon and pheasant swimming in cream soup. Any hunter of wild upland birds knows the taste of dry meat.

The little bit of fat that wild waterfowl carry, while not enough to need parboiling, will, however, flare up when cooked directly over charcoals or flame. The easiest way I've found to avoid fat fires is to move the pile of charcoal to one side of the grill, and the bird to the other, then close the lid. The same works for propane grills if you have two burners. Since barbecues are designed to imitate blast furnaces, at the lowest setting the minimum inside temperature will be 325° to 350° F (163° to 177° C). With one burner on high in a two-burner grill, you can still get a fast-cooked bird. If you have only one burner, keep the water pistol handy.

And if you really don't like the flavor of waterfowl fat, parboiling will only make sure it is totally rendered into the meat. You need to remove the skin. That's where most of the fat is. Then, make sure you don't keep them too long in the freezer. The flavor you object to may be the fat going rancid if you store ducks and geese longer than six to nine months.

• *"It's* big *game, isn't it? I don't need a lot."*

Around our neighborhood, the greeting during hunting season isn't "Good morning." It's "Got your elk yet?" It's not really hard to see why. A young deer in the freezer is about fifty pounds (23 kg) of boned meat, which is not enough to sustain even one person till the next hunting season. An elk, on the other hand, would feed two, if you didn't have too many dinner parties. Thus, getting your elk, *is* getting your meat.

For the rest of us—who don't have an elk, musk ox, or woolly mammoth tag—how do we tell how much is enough? Begin with a simple, four ounces (100 g) per person per day. A family of four needs one pound ($\frac{1}{2}$ kg) of meat a day, multiplied by the number of days you eat all your meals at home. My husband and I work at home, grabbing leftovers from the refrigerator as we work, so we probably throw the meals-eaten-out curve off. We also entertain quite a bit, and we buy very little commercial meat each year. Teenage boys also skew the curve. When my son Sean was a protein-hungry, fast-growing teen, there was no telling how much meat he would consume in a day. Whole roasts would disappear, and instead of sugar snacks he ate jerky. Four ounces (100 g) per day is the recommendation of the U.S. Heart Association and the USDA; he probably exceeded that by 400 percent.

Let's figure the average: a family of four and four dinners a week eaten at home; 40 pounds (18 kg) a week, fifty-two weeks a year. That's about 210 pounds (96 kg) of meat a year. That assumes you do not buy any other meat and that you eat only the recommended daily requirement. Add in the variations of your family—entertaining, a love of pork ribs, or a teenager in residence—and make your own estimate.

Then make an estimate of every animal you put in the freezer. If you are fortunate enough to pass by a fish and game weigh station, jot down the dressed weight of your animal (dressed weight being about 80 percent of live weight). You can also weigh the dressed animal on your home scale by quartering it and weighing all the parts in turn—but don't forget heads, hides, and horns. Then figure 35 to 40 percent of dressed weight: that will be your final boned weight. The sex, age, or species of the animal makes no difference. The rule is 35 to 40 percent.

An antelope (either sex) or whitetail or muley doe, weighing 80 to 90 pounds (36 to 41 kg) field dressed, average, will yield 30 to 35 pounds (14 to 16 kg) of boned meat. Mature whitetail and muley bucks, 170 pounds (77 kg) field dressed, yield about 60 pounds (27 kg) of pure meat. You don't have to bone out every animal. Butcher any way you want, but it helps to make an educated guess regarding edible meat. Personally, I hate the hollow sound of an empty freezer.

Because hunting is an inexact science at best, John and I plan on four deer-sized animals a year, then whatever else we are lucky enough to come by we add to the savings account. That's what I consider our second

The end of a successful whitetail hunt. (Photograph © John Barsness)

freezer—a savings account. You can have the best plans for hunting season, and then get called up for service in Saudi Arabia like Milo, or fall on a rock pile and wrench your back like Bill, or fall out of your Texas tree stand like Buck. One year I fell over a log on opening day of grouse season—rather than scratch my newly restocked Beretta Silver Snipe—and limped through Thanksgiving weekend. The next year, John broke his foot a week before the general rifle season started. If we couldn't hunt at all this year, we'd still have that second freezer, and we still wouldn't need to buy meat. That's the way we like to live, so we hunt and gather what we need, then a little more in case. If life insurance should be three times your yearly salary, I'd say freezer insurance should cover double your annual consumption.

• *"Hindquarters are the only good meat on game animals."*
This is one of my biggest pet peeves. The hindquarters provide the best steaks and dry-roasting meat. That part is true. Like all four-footed food animals—beef, as well as venison—the most tender meat comes off the highest part of the hindquarters. In a nation that defines meat as steak, some have taken that statement to mean the front quarters are worthless for anything but burger.

A lot of us, however, like something besides steak and potatoes every night. The brisket of larger game animals has traditionally been used for corning and for slow smoking with lots of barbecue sauce; rolled shoulder roasts can be slow roasted in a covered grill or water smoker; shoulder steaks can be as tender as any rib steak in the grocery store if the animal is young or just aged well; elk ribs can be slow cooked into a tasty, low-fat party appetizer or full-course meal. And necks, probably the piece of forward compartment meat that's most often ground into burger, make an incredibly moist and delicious pot roast. Have you ever heard the adage "the meat is sweeter closer to the bone?" Well, necks not only have lots of bone, they also have a little bit of fat embedded in the meat to baste the roast while it cooks.

The hindquarters may have the most tender meat, but, personally, I think the front quarters are tender enough and offer more flavor and more variety. If you dig deep enough in cooking literature, you'll discover that the best kept secret in beef cookery is that tenderloins are not nearly as tasty as other, lesser cuts. This is just as true with venison. I prefer a well-aged and well-cared-for shoulder steak to a tenderloin, and, in any event, I have found shoulder steaks to be quite tender

even on two-and-a-half-year-old bucks. I have nothing against those tender rear-quarter steaks, but venison offers a whole lot more.

And the unspoken myth:

• *"Women can't hunt."*
That's the biggest myth of all, and the debunking is in the hunting magazines: They say the best gentleman's rifle is the .30-06—or even the .338, but the best lady's rifle is the "diminutive" .243. Now who do you think would have to develop into the better hunter?

Let's encourage young girls to take hunter safety and have the same close relationship with their hunting fathers and mothers that boys have always been encouraged to share. The future of our hunting heritage is in our youth, all of our youth.

The Essentials—Fuel Cookers and the Kitchen Sink

These days, shopping for a barbecue comes with a bit of sticker shock. The old $20 hibachi is now a $100 charcoal kettle grill, or a $250 three-burner propane unit. But if you think that's expensive, add up the bill for a twenty-year supply of charcoal and lighter fluid, wood chips and chunks, smoker boxes, starter chimneys, and all the rest of the stuff that a very well-developed barbecue industry is telling us is absolutely necessary to grill a couple of burgers. Some of these items will, indeed, get used every day. Others quickly get relegated to the basement.

This is the perfect illustration of the adage that one person's treasure is another person's garbage. Starting with the cooker itself, and the fuels that fire it, and ending with what some might call wretched excess, here is a list of candidates for making barbecuing and grilling more pleasurable.

Note: The word "barbecue" can get confusing. As a noun, it is widely used as the term for any outdoor cooking device that you would grill steaks or burgers on. As a verb, it is most correct when referring to the long, slow cooking of tough cuts of meat that is practiced in Texas, Kansas City, the Carolinas, and places in between. But, just try to correct your brother when he uses the word barbecue, incorrectly, as a verb, as in "I'm going to go out on the patio and barbecue these steaks." Advertisement inserts in your paper and catalogs in your mailbox will refer to grills as barbecues, and to true barbecuing machines as smokers, which may cause consternation among barbecuing aficionados. But as long as you don't try to "grill" a tough brisket—and serve it to your family—this confusion is not life-threatening. Fast, hot cooking may be done on the "barbecue" you bought at Sears, but the process is grilling. Slow, relatively cooler, cooking—with or without smoke and moisture added—is barbecuing.

The Fuel

First, the argument for propane. It's clean; it's easy. Step out on the porch ten minutes before you want to start cooking, preheat the unit, and it's ready to go. No more recalcitrant chunks of charcoal dictating how long you must wait before starting dinner. No more lugging bags of charcoal, no more squirting lighter fluid, then having the fire not start and wondering if it's safe to squirt flammable liquid again so soon. Propane is also cheaper: Even if I barbecue every day, I use three or four small tanks a year—about $40. On the other hand, briquettes are $3 to $5 per ten-pound (5-kg) bag, and I'm always running out or replacing what gets rained on. One ten-pound (5-kg) bag makes two to three fires. (Actually, if my mom's starting the fire, it's only *one.)* Over 365 days, that's about 122 bags. Plus lighter fluid (if you don't use a charcoal chimney). I didn't need much convincing to switch from that old-fashioned, dirty charcoal to propane.

But like a lot of choices in life, it isn't that easy. For one thing, a lot of people still prefer the authentic outdoor taste of charcoal to propane. Then, too, the propane barbecue is its own worst enemy. Since it's patterned after a blast furnace, it is less versatile than charcoal. Even on a really cold day, turning the control knob to the lowest setting and choking the tank down as low as it will go, the lowest temperature I can get is about 250° F (121° C). That sounds low until you want to do something besides sear a steak. Low-temperature smoking is best at 90° F (32° C), hot smoking at about 180° F (82° C), and smoke cooking begins at 200° to 220° F (93° to 104° C).

I had a cheap garage-sale charcoal barbecue and threw it out when I bought the propane. But ten months later, when I wanted to smoke some pheasant sausage and slow cook a brisket, I bought myself a charcoal unit. This time I bought a good one, with a domed top, vents bottom and top, and a rack to hold the coals off the grill floor. The dome circulates the heat so the meat is cooked top and bottom; the vents dampen or spark the coals; the coal rack makes the vents more efficient. And the

charcoal? I can sear a steak with a big fire, or smoke sausages with a small fire. Gas is always advertised as offering infinite control, but in outdoor cooking, it's really the charcoal that has this benefit. So now I have both charcoal and propane units. I use the propane for the fast and lazy stuff and the charcoal for slower and more labor-intensive cooking.

Dry versus Wet

Aside from the two-burner propane unit and the charcoal kettle grill, I use the Little Chief aluminum smoker, which works at a constant 135° to 145° F (57° to 63° C) without any interference from me. I can smoke a fish in nine hours, venison salami in twelve, all with a minimum of work. This electric smoker also uses a very easily available wood for smoking—chips. A bag of chips and chunks costs about $1.50, and you can get it, the smoker, and its replacement parts at most sporting good stores.

As an aside, I should mention that there is also a Big Chief smoker, which looks like a really good deal at only 50 percent more money and twice the capacity. If you smoke large quantities of fish, fowl, and meats and can fill the Big Chief each time you use it, it is a good deal. If, however, you smoke less than twenty pounds (9.1 kg) of game at any one time, the Little Chief will work better. The Little Chief will maintain that ideal smoking temperature whether it is filled to capacity or only smoking one or two fish. The Big Chief, with its bigger amperage, is made to be operated at near or full capacity. Underfilled, it operates too hot. I own two Little Chiefs which, with my small family, works better than one big one.

I also bought an electric water smoker. After using it a few months, there were times I wished I'd bought a charcoal one, and times I was happy as a clam it was electric. It cooks at a constant 245° F (118° C), electrically, meaning I don't have to keep filling it with coals and monitoring the heat. But at that temperature I can't cool smoke. Propane water smokers suffer the same uncontrollability. And watch out when the water reservoir runs dry on either one. I've had the temperature spike to 350° F (177° C).

With a charcoal water smoker, on the other hand, you get infinite temperature control. The downside is that you have to monitor and feed it constantly, and unless you buy a very expensive water smoker, the built-in temperature gauge registers merely high, low, and medium—not actual temperatures. The extra attention

The perforated cast iron is great as an auxiliary cooking rack, the square hinged basket ideal for burgers and barbecued pizza, and the long basket perfect for kabobs.

you need to pay to the charcoal smoker can be worth the trouble. Foods that are cured and slow smoked last a lot longer than foods that are just smoke cooked, and some foods like brisket simply shouldn't be cooked above 200° F (93° C). Nevertheless, most meats that are smoke cooked and frozen or consumed immediately are just as good and don't take nearly as long to cook. But, you could've done all that on a well-vented charcoal kettle grill with the same temperature fire. The number of pros and cons to each method can make purchasing decisions difficult, to say the least. My response was to buy a variety of smokers for a variety of uses, including a second water smoker: a charcoal one.

What the water smoker adds is a large reservoir for liquids (from water to red wine and beer) and a domed top, which together provide a very effective moisture-infusing mechanism—perfect for low-fat game meats. Even a tough brisket will melt in your mouth when slow-cooked in a water smoker. I recently took two briskets and cooked one on my propane barbecue at 240° F (116° C) with a water pan to add moisture, and one on the water smoker. They both had very good flavor, and the propane brisket was tender, but it was the water-smoked brisket that could be shredded with a fork. I've also tried upland birds—with a little hickory smoke—and ribs. All came out of the water smoker noticeably more moist and tender.

Now, before you go out and buy a water smoker or two, I'll add that there are ways to imitate part of the water-smoke effect. Try this: Set your charcoal on one

side of the fire grate (or start one burner of your propane grill) and place an aluminum drip pan on the other side. Fill the drip pan with water. The fire will turn the water to steam as well as lower the temperature of the fire a few degrees, creating a pseudo–water smoker. Then add wood to the coals to complete the effect.

This is the method I used for the Tipsy Brisket recipe, and, because that recipe includes vinegar, the subterfuge works. The brisket comes out as tender as the other brisket recipes cooked in a genuine water smoker. For vinegar-less brisket recipes, and cooking whole geese and turkeys, however, nothing replaces a true water smoker. Whether you choose the convenience of electricity or propane, or the fine control of charcoal, a water smoker is a great addition to backyard cooking.

The Kitchen Sink

A lot of people think the initial cost of the cooker is the big expense in grilling and barbecuing. But if you bought one each of every auxiliary gadget on the market, you'd quickly change your mind. Here are the gadgets I find essential.

Charcoal chimneys

This was the first piece of paraphernalia I bought for my new charcoal grill. I had never felt comfortable with lighter fluid and had never been very good at starting briquettes. The chimney is just that: a metal cylinder that holds up to fifty briquettes—enough for a good, hot fire—and has an open top and a grate three inches (7 ½ cm) from the bottom. The coals sit on the grate. You stuff a couple of pieces of paper into the cylinder below the grate and light them with a match. It's the most efficient and predictable way to start charcoals I've found, costs only $10 to $12, and lasts a lifetime.

The second advantage to a charcoal chimney is that when you are smoking and need more than one hour of coals, you can start a second set of coals in the chimney while the first set starts smoking in the barbecue. Then, when the first fire starts to fall below 180° F (82° C), the second batch will be ready to go.

Burger grates and kabob baskets

One of my favorite side dishes is barbecued vegetables: Take whole plum tomatoes; then chunk up a bunch of raw onions and green peppers, precooked potatoes, and corn on the cob; marinate everything in a bit of oil, balsamic vinegar, and salt and pepper; then fill up the kabob baskets and grill them next to a couple of venison steaks.

I'm not being fancy. The truth is that chunks of meat will stay on those kabob sticks pretty well, but I'm tired of losing all those delicious grilled tomatoes and peppers just as they're reaching perfection. They simply don't have enough muscle to hang onto the skewers. A hinged hamburger grate, designed for beef burgers, will work just as well as the baskets for vegetables, and if you don't add suet to your ground venison, the grate is also the perfect solution for grilling crumbly venison burgers. It's a dilemma: Fat-added burgers don't fall through the slats of a grill rack, but straight ground venison is healthier. I like grilled burgers, so a hinged grate lets me have my cake and eat it too, so to speak.

You can do everything you used to do on your old skewers using hinged grates and baskets. You can still pre-assemble your dinner in the grate or basket and marinate it overnight; and you can still brush on all the sauce you want to while cooking. The spaces will allow all the good flavors to penetrate. The advantage is you'll lose less food to the bottom of the marinade bowl—and to the fire. Just be sure to brush or spray a little oil on whatever device you use to prevent sticking.

If skewers are still your tool of choice for grilling chunks of meat and vegetables, buy double-pronged or square-shafted skewers to grip the pieces better. Rounded skewers allow the food to rotate when you turn them, which means one side gets cooked twice, one not at all.

Tongs, spatulas, and the four flusher fork
The main advantage of cooking a steak over a hot fire is that you sear the outside of the meat very quickly—more quickly than your oven broiler—and seal in the juices. That's why even lesser cuts of meat taste better cooked outdoors. If you stick a fork in a piece of seared meat, either to turn it over or to remove it from the fire, you stick a hole in that nice sealing job and let the juices run out. Buy yourself a pair of long-handled tongs, or use a metal spatula on steaks and burgers. I save one pair of hot pads to hand-carry and hand-turn roasts. Never use a fork—never waste the juices you worked so hard to keep.

Aluminum drip pans
To prevent fat fires during direct cooking, you need to get pretty accurate with a water pistol. Or, set your meat on a drip pan, with or without a metal cradle, and ignore it. If the fat doesn't drip into the fire, there are

The larger the piece of wood, the slower and cooler it burns: Small chips, chips, and chunk each serve a purpose.

no flare-ups. For indirect cooking or smoking, lay a drip pan (slightly larger than the meat you are cooking) on the fire rack under the meat, then pile the coals on two sides of the pan. Or, light the fire on one side of the grill, and place the meat on the other side. Straight venison will not cause many fat fires, especially when you cook with the lid closed, but waterfowl, and any barded or larded meat (fat added on top or laced into the meat), and fat-added venison burgers will cause fat flare-ups, which will then scorch the meat much like a blow torch would. (And, according to some scare reports, scorching adds carcinogens to your repast.) Aluminum drip pans are cheap and disposable.

The wire brush
To prevent meat from sticking to the cooking surface, keep a wire brush handy to remove any crusty or charred bits before using the grill again. Lightly brush or spray oil on the cool rack—when it is off of the grill—and on accessory grates or baskets before each use.

Flavoring herbs and woods
A scattering of fresh herbs over the fire adds a delicate flavor to any meat while it's cooking. For a moderate flavor, use four or five 5-inch (13-cm) sprigs of any of your favorite fresh herbs. I like oregano with pheasant sausages and sage with antelope, but use the seasonings you like best. There are no rules for this kind of thing, and since it's such an easy act—throwing a branch or two on the fire—experiment. I wouldn't use dill on red meat or game birds, but oregano, sage, tarragon, basil,

A cast iron wood box can be set on the cooking rack of your propane or charcoal grill to add smoke to any meal.

summer savory, thyme, and marjoram would all work. Don't try wild sage; it's not really the same thing.

For a sharper or more traditional barbecue flavor use wood chips or chunks. There's a wide variety to choose from. In Montana stores, without resorting to catalog shopping, I've collected hickory, mesquite, alder, apple, cherry, osage, orange, grapevine, and pecan—in fine sawdust, chips, and chunks. The fruit woods are mellow tasting, the hickory has a bite. Mesquite, while it has a mythic reputation, is best for short, quick smoking—steaks rather than roasts, for instance.

No matter what wood you are using, small chips work best for quick, hot cooking over direct heat, but they're also the size needed in aluminum smokers to give the meat a quick infusion of smoke while it's still able to absorb it. Chips should be soaked thirty minutes in water before using. Chunks are best for longer cooking and are soaked for two to three hours in advance of their use. It's a simple equation: The larger the wood chunks the longer—and slower—the pieces smolder. Large chunks, two or three inches (5 or 7½ cm) thick, will

smoke for an hour. Use one chunk for light flavor, four for heavy. Chips smoke more intensely than chunks and last for twenty-five to thirty minutes.

On a charcoal fire, hot or warm, you can add fresh herbs or chunks of wood directly to the coals. In an electric water smoker, place the presoaked wood chunks on the fake coals, but be careful not to let them touch the electric element that lies exposed at the bottom of the smoker. (That leaves a very small, but sufficient area for the wood.) On a propane grill, if you set the wood directly on the fake coals, they will flare up. Manufacturers recommend placing the chunks inside a wood box to prevent any flare-up.

Follow the suggestions for both wood flavoring and herbs in this book, then adapt the intensity to your own tastes.

Setting the Fire

There are basically two kinds of fire: direct and indirect. Whether you use coals, electricity, or propane; grill, barbecue, or smoke, there's only direct and indirect. Direct fires are built directly under the food to be cooked; indirect fires are built to the side or sides. So now, you ask, what does this have to do with reality? It's simple.

Use a direct fire to cook small, thin, and tender pieces of meat, such as steaks, kabobs, pheasant breasts, and halved ruffed grouse.

Use an indirect fire to cook larger food that would char on the outside before the inside was finished: this includes roasts and turkeys. Use it also to avoid fat fires when cooking fatty foods: such as waterfowl and fat-added venison and bird sausages. Use an indirect fire also to cook tougher meats at a lower, slower temperature: good for briskets and ribs. Smoking uses indirect fire, as does the long and slow-cooking traditional barbecue.

To Set a Direct Fire

Preheat your propane for ten minutes. Or pile your briquettes in the middle of your barbecue and light with starter fluid. After thirty minutes, check your charcoal; it should have a white ash growing over the surface. (Alternately, start the coals in a charcoal chimney, without fluid, and after about fifteen minutes pour onto the fire rack.) When the coals are hot, spread them out in a single layer large enough to cook all your steaks and burgers at once. Most dinners need four dozen briquettes or less.

To Set an Indirect Fire

For propane you need a two burner unit. Light only one side, and preheat for ten minutes. For charcoal, pile the briquettes on one side of the fire rack and light. When hot, distribute on one side only of the coal rack. Set your meat on the other side of the cooking rack to cook it. Alternately, separate the fire into two equal parts, and push each to one side of center. Then place your meat in the center of the open cooking surface. You'll see both methods of coal dispersal used in this book.

How Hot is Hot?

Here's the easiest gauge I know. It works the same with any heat source.

• High: Hold your hand just over the cooking surface of the grill. If you can hold your hand there only two to three seconds, it is a hot fire. This is perfect for steaks—about five to six minutes a side—and for bird breasts of about 1- to 1½-inch (2½- to 4-cm) thickness. (An oven thermometer in a closed, high grill, would register over 500° F/260° C.)

• Medium: Hold your hand just over the cooking surface of the grill. If you can hold your hand there, comfortably, for four to five seconds, it's a medium fire. This temperature is also good for steaks, but it takes nearly twice as long. It's perfect for direct cooking of halved or whole birds more than 1½ inches (4 cm) thick and for indirect cooking of whole geese and roasts. (An oven thermometer in a closed, medium grill, would register about 350° F/177° C.)

• Low: Hold your hand just over the cooking surface of the grill. If you can hold your hand there for six to seven seconds, it's a low fire. It's still too hot for those traditional, long-cooked barbecued ribs and briskets, but it's good for hot smoking. If you aren't planning to hot smoke, then you need to pile the briquettes closer, open the dampers, or turn up the propane to increase the temperature. (An oven thermometer, left in a closed, low grill, would register about 250° F/121° C.)

Cautions

This list may sound sophomoric and redundant, and if it does, I'm happy. But, read it anyway. At some place and time, someone has forgotten one of these rules and ended up getting hurt. That's why they've made it into print.

1. Never use alcohol or gasoline in place of lighter fluid.
2. Never pour lighter fluid on hot coals.
3. Store lighter fluid away from the grill; keep the grill away from flammable materials.
4. Whether you are using propane or charcoal, keep the barbecue open when starting your fire.
5. Do not move a hot grill.
6. Always operate the grill outdoors, on a level surface.
7. If you are barbecuing on a combustible surface such as a wood deck, place a flame-resistant pad beneath the grill.
8. Beware of low-hanging tree limbs, roof overhangs, and any other flammable overhead material.
9. Keep small children and pets away from the barbecue. (Especially male dogs around low-slung electric water smokers. Enough said.)
10. Remove cooking racks from the barbecue before spraying with oil. Never spray hot surfaces. Never spray oil toward an open flame.

HOW SHOULD I COOK IT?

Keep these two rules in mind when you try to imagine what cut will go with what recipe. First, the general rule of thumb is that the most tender meat on all animals is high on the rump. Move forward or down and the meat gets relatively tougher. (On some animals it's all tender; others it's all tough. To determine the quality of your meat, do the shoulder steak test noted on page 10 in the "But when is it done aging?" section of the myth "Freezing a whole carcass ruins the meat." That way, you test the potentially toughest cut.) Second, tough cuts should be cooked at a low temperature with moisture; tender cuts are delicious cooked quickly, with no added moisture necessary.

But just because this is a barbecue book, don't assume you'll only be able to cook the tender cuts. Since wild meat is wild meat, I have made sure to include a good selection of recipes especially for tough and gamy meat. The following list notes those recipes that are especially kind to meat that is either tough or strong tasting.

Recipes for tough venison
Any venison sausage recipe
Barbecued Pizza
Inside-Out Chili Cheeseburgers
Kansas City–Style Barbecued Elk Ribs
Lazy-Day Ribs
Lazy Gourmet Burgers
The No-Suet-Added Burger
Low-Fat Carolina Elk Brisket
Mesquite-Smoked Twelve-Hour Fajita Jerky
Mr. Cholesterol Ribs
Melt-in-Your-Mouth Smoked Meatloaf
Stuff Burgers
Tipsy Brisket
Two-Hour Cheatin' Hickory Jerky
Venison Rolls

Recipes for tough birds
Alder-Smoked Turkey Salad
Any bird sausage recipe
Beer-Smoked Scaup
Cider Goose Breasts
Glazed Duck Legs
Pheasant in the Bag
Portly Prairie Grouse
Slow-Smoked Duck in Maple Ginger Glaze
Smothered Quail with Black Walnut Sauce
Spring-Cleaning Goose with Smoked Garlic Bread
Succulent Smoked Sage Grouse

Recipes for strong tasting venison
Barbecued Pizza
Bou Bobs
Inside-Out Chili Cheeseburgers
Kansas City–Style Barbecued Elk Ribs
Mesquite-Smoked Twelve-Hour Fajita Jerky
Venison Rolls

Recipes for strong tasting birds
August Andouille
Beer-Smoked Scaup
Chilled Pecan-Smoked Goose with Red Pepper
   Aioli
Golden Pheasant
Cider Goose Breast
Glazed Duck Legs
Goose Pepper Sausage
Peking Duck Sausage
Portly Prairie Grouse
Smothered Quail with Black Walnut Sauce
Succulent Smoked Sage Grouse

BIG GAME RECIPES

Ask me what kind of hunting I like best, and the first words out of my mouth will be "river-bottom whitetails." Sitting under an old cottonwood tree as light starts to wash over my corner of the world, I am the lone human observer of that wilderness intersection between owl night and hawk day. I loved bow hunting for river-bottom whitetails—until my rotator cuff couldn't take it any more—because the warmer September weather was more conducive to afternoon naps in the field than those sometimes frigid November afternoons rifle season has in store for us. And mid-afternoon naps, propped up against a gnarled and twisted fence post, are the best way I've found to make those suspicious does forget you are around. It's also a good way to count feral cats, foxes, and coyotes that are generally all but invisible.

But if that were the only way I could hunt, I'd miss climbing into the mountains behind my house the day after the first good snow looking for elk, sitting quietly in the whitetail woods, and taking long walks for antelope and mule deer out on the Great American Desert. One year was more distracting than most when, as I aimed at one 14-inch (36-cm) antelope buck, a flight of 2,000 sandhill cranes, flanked by 3,000 Canada geese, honked and whistled overhead. As I was about to catch my breath again and pull the trigger, my husband nudged me into the realization that a 5x5 muley buck was watching the spectacle himself, from the bluff above.

I like hunting alone best, unless I can hunt with good friends who shoot straight and carry more interesting lunches than I do. Last summer I hunted in Africa, shooting a gemsbok, red hartebeest, blue wildebeest, and kudu, with lunches prepared by a graduate of a South African culinary school. Her zebra burgers, hartebeest curry, and kudu cordon bleu dinners were wonderful, but lunch was my favorite meal. Avocado sandwiches, red bush tea, and biltong (the African version of jerky) sure beat my usual hunting lunch of liverwurst, Gatorade, and Milky Ways.

But I didn't get to bring my animals home, and no matter how good the friends and the lunches, the point—with me—always is to fill the freezer. That's the thing with big game: You *do* fill the freezer.

Here are some of my favorite recipes for big game animals that make our table fare varied and delicious. I hope they will become your favorites, too.

Page 25: *A Roosevelt elk in the redwoods. (Photograph © Jeffrey Rich Nature Photography)*

A large mule deer buck taken toward the end of the rut is often a candidate for moderately to highly spiced dishes. (Photograph © Michael H. Francis)

Steaks

The Elementary Steak

Perhaps nothing symbolizes the barbecue as much as the beef steak, and there is no reason in the world the venison steak can't be just as good. Sure, venison has less fat than a beef steak, but so does chicken. That has never stopped anyone from barbecuing a chicken.

There are a few basic things to remember, though. First, don't cut any steak destined for the barbecue any thinner than 1–1½ inches (2½–3¾ cm) thick. Second, cook the meat over a hot fire, directly over the coals, so the outside of the steak is seared quickly, thus sealing in the juices. Third, never turn steaks or any other cuts by stabbing a fork into them, and don't ever place them unoiled on a hot grill. The former will puncture, and the latter will tear open the steaks when you turn them, releasing all those juices you sealed in in the first place.

Last but not least, remember that the most common error in cooking game—and most other—meat is overcooking. Cooking time is determined by the thickness of the cut, not the total weight. A 1-inch (2½-cm) steak takes just 10–12 minutes to go from raw to medium whether it is a 1-pound (½ kg) steak or a 4 ouncer (100 g). That's not a very long time, especially when you consider you've got to remember to turn the steak halfway through the cooking. Now we're down to 5–6 minutes. Six minutes is how long it takes me to load my two Labs and three bags of duck decoys when the northern geese have arrived. Watch your watch; set a timer.

For a 1-inch (2½ cm) steak: Preheat a propane grill for 10 minutes, then turn down to high to cook. Or start 4 dozen charcoal briquettes and wait 25 minutes. The cooking surface should be hot: You should be able to hold your hand at cooking level for 4–5 seconds only.

Brush or wipe the steak with oil (or alternately brush or wipe the rack with oil, but only when it is cold). Place the steak on the grill, turn after 5 minutes, cook 5 minutes more, then remove it from the grill. If you are unsure, put a test steak on the grill with the dinner steaks. The test steak can be just 1–2 ounces (25–60 g), as long as it is the same thickness. After cooking 4 minutes a side, slice open the test steak, and it should be quite rare. Then you can adjust your cooking time for the other steaks to have them come out just the way you want them.

A 1½-inch (3¾-cm) steak, illogically, does not take 50 percent longer to cook than a 1-inch (2½-cm) steak. Allow only one minute more a side, then check the test steak. After all, barbecuing is still an inexact system of cooking. That's its charm, isn't it?

Is your mouth watering yet? Here are some of my favorite recipes.

To Grill Fresh Vegetables

For delicate vegetables—including tomatoes, mushrooms, asparagus, onions, peppers, and zucchinis—wash and trim them as you would to cook indoors, then place them on a lightly oiled grill at medium heat, turning once, cooking until fork tender, about 5–10 minutes.

For denser vegetables, such as carrots and potatoes, precook until fork tender by parboiling 5–10 minutes or microwaving for 4 minutes at 500 watts (2½ minutes at 700 watts). Then place on the grill and cook as above.

Whatever vegetables you use, you can grill them plain or baste with sauce either while cooking or just after you take them off the grill. Plain butter or a combination of butter, garlic powder, pepper, and grated Parmesan cheese is wonderful on almost any vegetable.

BLACK-AND-BLUE CHEESE STEAKS

Yield: 6 servings

It's the simple, basic steak cooked over the barbecue. But, ahead of time, in your leisure, make the blue cheese and nut butter, and dinnertime will be slightly less hectic.

Black-and-Blue Cheese Steaks

Ingredients

6 ounces (150 g) blue cheese, crumbled (1 ⅓ cups/320 ml)

4 tablespoons butter, softened

¼ cup (60 ml) chopped smokehouse almonds

1 ½ pounds (¾ kg) round steaks, cut 1 inch (2 ½ cm) thick

½ teaspoon salt

½ teaspoon pepper

Preparation

Up to 2 days ahead, combine the cheese and butter in a small bowl. Stir to blend. Gently fold in the almonds. Cover and refrigerate.

Cooking

1. Brush or wipe a light coating of oil on the cooking grate to prevent sticking.

2. Preheat a propane barbecue for 10 minutes, then turn down to medium high. Or start 40 charcoal briquettes, and wait 25 minutes. When the coals have a light coating of ash, and you can't hold your hand over them for more than 4–5 seconds, start the steaks.

3. Pat the steaks dry with paper towels. Season with salt and pepper, then place on the grill. Cook 10–12 minutes rare to medium rare; do not cook to medium. Venison is much more tender when there is still a little red in the center. Place a dollop of the blue cheese mixture on top of the hot steaks and serve with grilled vegetables.

SPICE-CRUSTED ELK STEAKS

Yield: 4 servings

No pounding, no marinating, no long cooking. Tender, sweet, round steaks are perfect for the barbecue. If you want to up the tender quotient, slice a boned tenderloin into a string of medallion steaks; this will make you put away the steak knives for good.

Spice-Crusted Elk Steaks

Ingredients
1 pound (½ kg) round steak, cut 1 inch (2½ cm) thick
1 teaspoon salt
¼ teaspoon granulated garlic powder
½ teaspoon whole black peppercorns
⅛ teaspoon crushed red pepper flakes
⅛ teaspoon whole celery seed
¼ teaspoon paprika

Cooking
1. Preheat a propane barbecue for 10 minutes, then turn down to high. Or start 4 dozen charcoal briquettes, wait 25 minutes, and when you can't hold your hand at cooking level for more than 4–5 seconds the coals are ready.

2. While the barbecue heats up, trim the steak and dry it with paper towels. Then wipe or brush on a light coating of oil. In a small bowl, combine the salt, garlic powder, peppercorns, red pepper flakes, celery seeds, and paprika. Crush the seasonings in a blender or with a rolling pin.

3. Sprinkle half of the seasonings on one side of the steak, then place the steak on the grill, spice side down. Brush the second side of the steak with oil, then sprinkle the rest of the spice mix over it. Leave the barbecue uncovered and cook 10–12 minutes for rare to medium rare, 15 minutes overall for medium, turning once halfway through the cooking. Serve with new potatoes and peas.

VENISON ROLLS

Yield: 18–20 rolls

Here's a great appetizer for those who love the hot stuff. The rolls are pounded so thin, they cook very fast. Put them on the grill just before cooking the main course. When the fire is just ready, then take them off the grill, sit back, and enjoy while the main course grills at a more leisurely pace.

A whitetail buck, out for an evening stroll. (Photograph © William H. Mullins)

Ingredients
1 pound (½ kg) shoulder steaks
2 teaspoons dried leaf oregano
1 teaspoon ground cumin
4-ounce can (100 g) mild whole jalapeño
    peppers
1 teaspoon salt
½ teaspoon pepper

Preparation
1. Dry the steaks with a paper towel, and pound with a meat mallet until very thin (about ¼ inch/½ cm). (For the sake of cleanliness and to prevent the steaks from tearing, lay a length of plastic wrap over the steaks before you begin tenderizing.) Cut the steaks into strips approximately 1½ inches (3¾ cm) wide and 4½– 5 inches (11½–12¾ cm) long. Set aside. In a small bowl combine the oregano and cumin.
2. Drain the liquid off the jalapeños and cut them into the same number of pieces as you have steak strips. (There's usually three jalapeños to a can.) Then roll the pepper pieces in the oregano and cumin mixture, place each piece at one end of a tenderized steak strip, roll the pepper up into the steak, and secure the roll with a toothpick. Sprinkle each roll with some of the salt and pepper.

Cooking
Start 40 briquettes, or preheat a propane barbecue and turn down to medium high heat. When the charcoals are white hot, and you can only hold your hand at cooking level for 4–5 seconds, place the rolls on the grill directly over the coals. Cook about 3–4 minutes to a side— 6–8 minutes total. Serve as an appetizer, with chips and salsa.

Whitetail Bruschetta Heroes

Yield: 4 servings

Here's the perfect solution to leftover steaks and roasts. Chilled and delicious, open-faced bruschetta is an easy Italian classic. As with all cuts (except jerky), slice across the diagonal for more tender eating.

Whitetail Bruschetta Heroes

Ingredients

4 ripe Roma or plum tomatoes, diced
6 cloves garlic, minced
4 tablespoons minced red onion
½ cup (125 ml) olive oil
½ cup (125 ml) vinegar (rice wine vinegar is best)
½ teaspoon pepper
2 French rolls, each 8 inches long
1 pound (½ kg) leftover steak, thinly sliced
¼ cup (60 ml) grated Parmesan cheese

Preparation

In a medium-sized bowl, combine the tomatoes, garlic, onion, oil, vinegar, and pepper. Stir gently, then cover and refrigerate. Slice the French rolls in half lengthwise.

Cooking

1. Preheat a propane barbecue for 10 minutes, then turn the heat down to medium. Lightly brush the rolls with oil, then turn oil side down on the grill. Cook about 3 minutes, until golden brown.

2. Spoon the tomato mixture onto the rolls, then lay the steak slices across the bruschetta and sprinkle with Parmesan cheese. Makes a delightfully different leftover lunch, or you can cut them into smaller sections and serve as an appetizer.

Recipe note: If you don't have any leftovers around, make the Elementary Steak (see recipe on page 28), rare to medium rare, then chill before assembly.

SWEET-AND-SOUR ELK STEAKS

Yield: 4 servings

The sweet-and-sour sauce for these steaks is very intense, so I prefer only 1 tablespoon per steak. If you want more, simply double the recipe.

Sweet-and-Sour Elk Steaks

Ingredients

5 tablespoons red currant jelly

2 tablespoons stone-ground mustard

1 tablespoon minced green onion (greens only)

$\frac{3}{4}$ teaspoon ground lemon peel

4 elk round steaks, 6-ounces (150 g) each

2 tablespoons butter, melted

1 teaspoon salt

$\frac{1}{2}$ teaspoon pepper

Preparation

In a microwavable bowl or double boiler, liquefy the currant jelly. Add the mustard, onion, and lemon peel and set aside. (You can make the sauce ahead and store it in the refrigerator, then reheat it just before using. The jelly will not set up again when chilled.)

Cooking

1. Preheat a propane barbecue for 10 minutes, then turn down to high to cook. Or start 4 dozen charcoal briquettes, wait 25 minutes, and when the coals are so hot you can't hold your hand more than 4–5 seconds at cooking level, the fire is ready.

2. While the grill heats up, dry the steaks with a paper towel. Just before you put them on the grill, brush one side with the butter and season with half the salt and pepper. Place the 4 steaks on the grill, butter side down, then brush and season the top sides. Cook about 5 minutes a side for rare, 6–7 for medium.

3. Transfer the steaks to dinner plates and spoon some of the sweet-and-sour sauce over each one. Serve with corn relish and macaroni and cheese.

Recipe note: This sweet-and-sour sauce can be served warm, as with the steaks in this recipe, or it can be chilled and spread on steak sandwiches, as you would use cranberry sauce on leftover turkey sandwiches.

CHILI ON A STICK

Yield: 6 servings

Summertime and the kitchen is hot—too hot to make chili. Unless you make chili on a stick. And use that randy old whitetail that doesn't taste very good, if that's all you have. The marinade will soothe all but the most gamy flavors.

Ingredients

2 pounds (1 kg) shoulder steaks
¾ cup (185 ml) red wine vinegar
½ cup (125 ml) apple juice
½ cup (125 ml) vegetable oil
¼ cup (60 ml) minced onion
2 cloves garlic, minced
½ teaspoon chili powder
1 teaspoon dried leaf cilantro (or 1 tablespoon chopped fresh cilantro)
½ teaspoon salt
1 teaspoon black pepper
6 fresh, whole jalapeño peppers
12 large-bulbed green onions
1 pound (½ kg) cherry tomatoes
½ cup (125 ml) mesquite wood chips

Preparation

1. Trim the steaks of all fat and sinewy material, then pat dry with paper towels. In a glass bowl or resealable plastic bag, combine the marinade ingredients: vinegar, apple juice, oil, onion, garlic, chili powder, cilantro, salt, and black pepper. Stir, then add the steaks. Place the marinating steaks in the refrigerator, covered or sealed, for 2–4 hours.

2. When the first hour is up, put the mesquite wood chips in a pail of water, and prepare the vegetables for the skewers. Wearing rubber gloves, cut off the tops of the jalapeños and core and seed them. Cut them in half lengthwise. Trim the tops and bottoms of the onions, leaving about 3 inches (7½ cm) of green tops. Drain the meat, cut it up into 1–2 inch (2½–5 cm) chunks, and alternate the meat, onion, jalapeños, and tomatoes on the skewers. Begin and end with the meat to secure the stringer.

Cooking

1. For a propane barbecue: Drain the wood chips and place them in a wood box. Set it on one side of the coal grate. Preheat the unit for 10 minutes, then turn down to medium high heat. For charcoal: Start 40 charcoal briquettes on one side of the grill, wait 25 minutes, then spread them out in a single layer, leaving room in the middle to nestle the wood box among the coals.

2. Place the kabobs over the hot coals, and not directly over the wood chips. Cover the grill and cook 8–10 minutes, basting often and turning once. Serve with lots of chips and Mexican beer in well-chilled glasses.

Chili on a Stick

OF SINEW, FAT, AND SILVER SKIN:
TRIMMED (AND TASTY) VENISON

When my husband and I butcher a deer, elk, moose, or any other venison animal, he cuts the roasts, steaks, and stew meat off the bone while I do the trimming. Then, when he's done, he wraps, labels and carts the trimmed meat off to the basement freezer—as I start trimming the meat destined for the grinder.

Do I take forever to perform my "half" of the job? Yes. But careful trimming—before freezing—is crucial to the cook's success.

In the first place, fat—no matter the source—doesn't store long in the freezer despite how well you wrap it—and fat is one of the places gamy flavors are stored. Gristle, sinew, and silver skin (a delicate white film found directly over muscle meat) are others. If any part of the animal tastes even the slightest bit gamy when you first put it in the freezer, watch out when you take it back out for dinner. It seems impossible, but gamy flavors only get gamier the longer they stay in the freezer. As bad as that is, gaminess also affects the texture of connective tissue, leaving the gristle all but inedible after a few weeks.

Sure, you could trim the bad stuff off after it's been thawed again, but by then the flavors have begun to spread into the meat. Or you could just plow through the gamy stuff to get to the good stuff. But the longer you avoid those carefully wrapped time bombs in your freezer, the worse they get.

To limit the bad flavor's effect on your next meal, it is necessary to be ruthless in your trimming. In the end, you will waste less and spend less time doctoring and coping with your wild venison.

As you butcher, remove all outer fat and connective tissue, as well as damaged and dried meat, from the quarters. Then, once the steaks, roasts, etc. are cut, trim them again. Naturally, the gamier the animal, the more ruthless you need to be. With good tasting animals you need only remove what fat and connective tissue you see on the outside of the cut; no need to decimate that sweet tasting rump roast. But with gamy meat, trim, trim, trim. Solid muscle meat should still taste good, with a little help from the cook, so trim away anything else that isn't a healthy, deep red in color. A soup, stew, or chili made from good tasting solid meat is always more enjoyable than suffering through a roast that's been left untrimmed.

BOU BOBS

Yield: 4 servings

Use caribou, mule deer, or whitetail, but use an adult animal—two years old or more. Mature animals have a more complex flavor and firmer texture to the meat, which the red wine vinegar and soy sauce complement. Make sure, however, that the meat you use is tender. Kabobs cook very fast, and there's no time for tenderizing.

Ingredients
1 pound (½ kg) tender caribou
¼ cup (60 ml) red wine vinegar
¼ cup (60 ml) soy sauce
¼ cup (60 ml) vegetable oil
1 teaspoon ground lemon peel
½ teaspoon pepper

Preparation
Dry the caribou meat off with a paper towel, and cube it into 2-inch (5-cm) chunks. In a large bowl or resealable plastic bag, combine the red wine vinegar, soy sauce, oil, lemon peel, and pepper. Add the meat cubes, cover or seal, and marinate 24 hours in the refrigerator.

Cooking
1. Start 40 briquettes, or preheat a propane barbecue and turn down to medium high heat. Meanwhile, drain off and save the marinade. Pat the caribou chunks dry with paper towels, then place on skewers.
2. When the charcoals are white hot, and you can only hold your hand at cooking level for 4–5 seconds, lightly brush the meat chunks with the marinade and place on the grill. Cook about 5 minutes a side, then serve hot with risotto.

WHICH COOKING OIL IS BEST?

You'll notice some recipes in this book call for olive or canola oil, while others leave the choice up to you. That's not a mistake. All cooking oils are not alike. At our house we use a lot of olive oil, because many doctors believe the mono-unsaturated fat is actually good for your heart. We also use canola oil a lot because it is almost as high in mono-unsaturates as olive oil but has a higher smoking point. In the cupboard, behind these two staples, I also keep peanut oil for deep frying. It is high in saturated fats, but it also has the highest smoking point of readily available oils. That means you can fry some delicate, low-fat tidbit faster than it can absorb the oil it's floating in. And, even though the oil is operating at very hot temperatures, it will not leave your food with a burned flavor or deposit burned, black bits into the pan.

But what does this have to do with barbecuing, grilling, and smoking? In recipes where the heat on the grill is turned up high, I've suggested using canola oil so you don't get a burned taste in your food; in recipes where the oil is eaten without benefit of cooking, and the taste of the oil itself is really important (as in the Whitetail Bruschetta Heroes) I've suggested olive oil. Other places where the oil gets cooked with the meat, and high temperature isn't an issue, any liquid vegetable oil your family likes will work.

And then there's butter. Very low smoking point, but incredible flavor. Here and there in this book, butter is added after the cooking to take advantage of its rich flavor without having to deal with it charring on a really hot grill. If your family can't live without the full-fat flavor of beef, wiping a little butter on your venison steaks while they're grilling will go a long way to satisfy that hunger. That's something I do for special occasions, and special guests. A few meals here and there won't hurt. Just ignore the diet police.

TAKE CARE WITH MARINADES

Besides adding flavor and moisture to meats, marinades are reuseable. You can use them 3–4 times, over the course of a week, for marinating other meats—as long as you keep it refrigerated.

Or you can double dip at one meal—using the marinade for a sauce at the table—as long as you take one precaution. Once your meat is on the grill, pour the marinade off into a saucepan and bring it to a boil; lower the heat, and cook at a low boil for 4 minutes. This ensures that any bacteria present in the raw meat (commercial as well as wild) will not make its way, alive, to your plate.

FUR AND FEATHER KABOBS

Yield: 4–6 servings

Make these kabobs with your own homemade Whitetail Italian Sausage (see recipe on page 109), or substitute some from the store. The combination of white meat, red meat, and sausage is something worth lighting up the barbecue for. If you use wooden skewers, be sure to soak them in water 30 minutes before assembling the kabobs so the skewers won't burn up on the grill.

Ingredients

$\frac{1}{2}$ pound ($\frac{1}{4}$ kg) Whitetail Italian Sausage
$\frac{1}{2}$ pound ($\frac{1}{4}$ kg) pheasant breast
$\frac{1}{2}$ pound ($\frac{1}{4}$ kg) venison steak
1 sweet red pepper
1 sweet yellow pepper
$\frac{1}{2}$ cup (125 ml) olive or canola oil
Juice of 2 lemons
$\frac{1}{4}$ cup (60 ml) fresh, minced sage leaves
1 teaspoon salt
$\frac{1}{2}$ teaspoon pepper

Preparation

1. Cut the sausage, pheasant, and venison into 1-inch ($2\frac{1}{2}$-cm) cubes. Core and cube the peppers into 1-inch ($2\frac{1}{2}$-cm) pieces. Thread the meat and sweet peppers alternately onto the skewers.
2. In a shallow baking pan, lay the loaded skewers out in a single layer. Combine the oil, lemon juice, sage leaves, salt, and pepper in a small bowl, stir, and pour over the kabobs. Cover and refrigerate 1–2 hours.

Cooking

1. Preheat a propane barbecue for 10 minutes, then turn the heat down to medium high. Or start 40 charcoal briquettes and wait 25 minutes. When you cannot keep your hand at cooking level for more than 4–5 seconds, the coals are ready.
2. Drain the kabobs and transfer them to the barbecue. Cook directly over the coals, 5–6 minutes a side, until the sausage has no pink inside. (Remember the sausage must be cooked well, because of the pork in it.) Transfer to a serving platter, garnish with a few more sage leaves, and serve with garlic bread and fresh garden salad.

BURGERS

The Elementary Burger

1. Grinding and Mixing

If you do your own butchering and grinding, venison burger comes in at least three varieties: straight ground venison; straight ground venison with ground beef suet; straight ground venison with beef hamburger. If you use a commercial processor, you can request no fat in your burger mix, or as much fat as you want. The fat ratio we seek in our food is a matter of taste. To be sure your family will enjoy eating venison every day, it will help to keep the fat content of your venison burger at the same level you are used to eating in other meats.

The ground beef at the supermarket ranges from 27 to 5 percent fat (marked 73 to 95 percent lean). If you are used to buying 95 percent lean beef burger, add 5 percent beef suet to your ground venison, that is, to each 5 pounds (2½ kg) of venison, add 4 ounces (100 g) of suet. (Don't ask me where the 4-plus percent of fat inherent in venison goes, but this ratio from beef to venison burger tastes about the same.) As a last resort, a 50/50 ground venison with beef hamburger combination will probably be accepted without questions by even the most stringent of palates. With any of the recipes in this cookbook, you can use whatever form of ground venison your family will eat.

Year in and year out, I prefer the straight ground venison and have found that if I add 2 teaspoons of oil (olive or canola to keep it healthy) to each pound of ground

A burger grate makes for easier handling, especially when you don't add suet to your grinder.

meat, it will not crumble on the grill. Complete instructions follow in the No-Suet-Added Burger recipe (see below).

2. Cooking

Extensive scientific research has shown that the perfect burger is 4 inches (10 cm) in diameter, 1 inch (2½ cm) thick, and is loosely molded with the hands. That will qualify it as a hamburger rather than a hockey puck or miniature clay bird. To keep the patty from sticking to the grill, brush or wipe a very light coating of oil on the top and bottom of the patty, or alternately, on the cooking rack (but only when it is cool, or removed from the lit grill).

Finally, for the perfect finish, place it on a grill so hot that you cannot hold your hand more than 4–5 seconds at cooking level, and cook 7 minutes to a side. This provides you with a medium-cooked burger. If you have ground your own burger, being vigilant about cleanliness, and have not added commercially ground beef suet, you can safely cook your burger a little less—5 minutes to a side, for rare to medium rare. That is the advantage of grinding your own venison and keeping it lean. (But do remember to add 2 teaspoons of oil per pound to keep it from crumbling.)

Now that you have the nuts and bolts, here are a few recipes for ground meat.

THE NO-SUET-ADDED BURGER

Yield: 4 servings

For me, it's the constant conflict. How to grill a patty of straight ground venison—with no suet added—without having it crumble through the grate. You can put foil down, but the burger doesn't quite taste like it was barbecued. And not everyone has a hinged grate or a perforated cast iron grill. But everyone has a little canola or olive oil in the cupboard.

Ingredients

1½ pounds (¾ kg) ground venison
3 teaspoons vegetable oil

Cooking

1. Brush or lightly wipe a small amount of oil on the grill to prevent sticking. Preheat the propane barbecue then turn to medium high heat for cooking. Or start 40 briquettes and wait 25 minutes, until the coals are so hot you can't keep your hand at cooking surface more than 4–5 seconds.

2. While the grill heats, combine the ground venison and oil in a large bowl, mix thoroughly with your hands, and shape loosely into 4 patties, 1 inch (2½ cm) thick. The patties will weigh about 6 ounces (150 g).

3. Place the patties on the cooking rack, and cook 5 minutes to a side for rare, 7–8 minutes for medium. Serve in hamburger buns with ketchup and raw onions, with chips on the side.

STUFF BURGERS

Yield: 4 servings

They're Stuff Burgers not because they're stuffed with anything but because you can do so much stuff with them. They're a main course for a Wednesday night pick-me-up, a bright appetizer for your holiday dinner, or the main ingredient in a Saturday afternoon meatball hoagie. Follow the serving suggestions at the end of the recipe, or make up your own variations.

Stuff Burgers

Ingredients

3 green bell peppers
1½ cups (375 ml) cooked instant rice or couscous
3 ounces (75 g) grated mozzarella cheese
¼ cup (60 ml) grated Parmesan cheese
¾ teaspoon salt
¾ teaspoon pepper
1½ teaspoons dried leaf basil
1½ pounds (¾ kg) burger
2 egg whites

Preparation

1. Turn the green peppers stem side down on a cutting board. You will see 4 cusps—12, 3, 6, and 9 o'clock. Place your knife in the valley between the cusps and quarter the peppers, so each section is a canoe. (Actually, a pirogue, a wide-bodied canoe used by some Native American groups and made famous by the Lewis and Clark expedition.) Cut those 4 lengths in half crosswise. Now the pepper chunks should look like the back half of a pirogue.

2. In a large bowl, combine the rice, mozzarella cheese, all but 1 tablespoon of the Parmesan cheese, the salt, pepper, and basil. Stir. Now add the burger and the egg whites and mix thoroughly by hand. Shape the burger mix into 24 balls (about 1 tablespoon each) and stuff one into each of the half-pirogues, pressing it firmly into the vagaries of the inside of the pirogue. (These irregularities will help keep the burger in the boat.)

Cooking

1. Preheat a propane barbecue for 10 minutes then turn it down to medium heat. Or start 40 charcoal briquettes, wait 25 minutes, and start cooking when you can't hold your hand at cooking level more than 5–6 seconds.

2. Place the pirogues on the grill, stuffing side up, and cook about 10–12 minutes. Do not turn them over or you will lose the stuffing. The Stuff Burgers are done when the peppers start to blacken or wilt (depending on how close the peppers are to the fire), and are fork tender, and when the burger stuffing has no sign of red in the center. Serve as appetizers, or grill up a few very ripe tomatoes and pile everything into a hoagie roll. Instant meatball wedgies.

INSIDE-OUT CHILI CHEESEBURGERS

Yield: 4 servings

Hungry for cheeseburgers, but the cheese always runs into the fire? Try putting the cheese inside.

Inside-Out Chili Cheeseburgers

Ingredients
2 pounds (1 kg) burger
1 teaspoon salt
½ teaspoon pepper
¼ cup (60 ml) Cheez Whiz
4 teaspoons bottled chili sauce

Preparation
1. Preheat the propane barbecue for 10 minutes, then turn to high for cooking. Or start 4 dozen charcoal briquettes and wait 25 minutes for the coals to be so hot you can't hold your hand at cooking surface for more than 4–5 seconds.
2. While the barbecue heats up: In a large bowl, combine the burger with the salt and pepper and mix thoroughly. Divide the burger in thirds. Take two thirds of the burger and shape that into 4 patties, about 1 inch (2½ cm) thick. Press an indentation with your thumb into the center of each patty, about halfway down.
3. In a small bowl, combine the Cheez Whiz and the chili sauce and stir. Spoon an equal portion of the cheese mixture into the thumb mark of each patty. Now with the last third of the burger make a lid, place one on each patty, then gently press the patty all around until the cheese is sealed in.

Cooking
Place the patties on the grill, lid side up, and cook about 10 minutes to a side. (These take longer than the No-Suet-Added Burgers because the lid makes them thicker.) Serve with refried beans and corn chips.

LAZY GOURMET BURGERS

Yield: 4 servings

If you're like me, you have a few favorite dishes you make over and over. It's partly because they're easy, and partly because the whole family likes them. Well, here's a new favorite to add to your repertoire. And the only thing faster is a TV dinner.

Ingredients

2–3 medium-sized red onions, sliced $\frac{1}{2}$ inch (1 $\frac{1}{4}$ cm) thick
$\frac{1}{4}$ pound ($\frac{1}{8}$ kg) mushrooms, halved
1 green pepper, cut into eighths
$\frac{1}{4}$ cup (60 ml) olive or canola oil
$\frac{1}{2}$ teaspoon salt
$\frac{1}{2}$ teaspoon ground black pepper
$\frac{1}{3}$ cup (80 ml) dry red wine
1 tablespoon stone-ground mustard
1 teaspoon dried leaf thyme
1 bay leaf
1 teaspoon salt
6 whole black peppercorns
1 $\frac{1}{2}$ pounds ($\frac{3}{4}$ kg) burger
4 deli rolls

Preparation

In a large bowl, combine the onion, mushrooms, and green pepper. Pour the oil, salt, and ground black pepper over them and set aside. In a blender or food processor, combine the red wine, mustard, thyme, bay leaf, salt, and peppercorns. Process a few seconds till the pepper is cracked and the bay leaf crumbled. Pour into a separate large bowl, add the burger, and mix thoroughly. Shape the burger mix into patties, 1 inch (2 $\frac{1}{2}$ cm) thick.

Cooking

1. Lightly spray or rub the cooking rack with a small amount of oil. Preheat a propane barbecue for 10 minutes, then turn to medium high heat. Or start 40 charcoal briquettes and wait 25 minutes until the coals are so hot you can't keep your hand at the cooking surface for more than 4–5 seconds.
2. Place the burgers on the grill, and cook 10–12 minutes for rare, or 15 minutes for medium, turning once halfway through.
3. During the last 3–4 minutes of cooking, remove the onion slices, mushrooms, and peppers from the oil and place them on the grill. Turn frequently with a tong or spatula, then remove them with the burgers. Serve each burger in a deli roll, with a slice of grilled onion and a good portion of the mushrooms and peppers on top.

Melt-in-Your-Mouth Smoked Meat Loaf

Yield: 4–6 servings

If you absolutely can't eat meat loaf without sauce, add it in the last 30 minutes of cooking. But trust me. This meat loaf is so moist and juicy, you don't need any sauce.

Ingredients

3 chunks hickory
1 cup (250 ml) chopped onion
½ cup (125 ml) chopped green bell pepper
4 cloves garlic, minced
1 tablespoon vegetable oil
½ teaspoon ground cumin
½ teaspoon salt
1 teaspoon black pepper
1½ pounds (¾ kg) burger
¼ cup (60 ml) sour cream
1 egg
1 cup (250 ml) bread crumbs
½ cup (125 ml) cornmeal
2 tablespoons Worcestershire sauce
1 tablespoon green (not red) jalapeño pepper sauce
1 teaspoon beef bouillon granules
½ cup (125 ml) hot water

Preparation

1. Two hours before you want to start cooking, place the hickory chunks in a pail of water.

2. In a skillet, over medium heat, sauté the onion, green peppers, and garlic in the oil. Stir in the cumin, salt, and pepper and continue to cook until the vegetables have softened. Transfer them to a large bowl.

3. Add the burger, sour cream, egg, bread crumbs, cornmeal, Worcestershire sauce, and green jalapeño pepper sauce. Dissolve the bouillon granules in the hot water and add this broth to the meat mixture. Stir thoroughly with your hands and press into a barbecue-proof loaf pan.

Cooking

1. To cook in an electric water smoker: Drain the wood chunks and set them on the coals, then fill the reservoir with water. Place the meat loaf in the center of the lower rack, cover the smoker, and plug it in. For a charcoal smoker: Start 30–35 coals and wait 25 minutes. Adjust the vents and the position of the coals to get a constant 220°– 240° F (105°– 115° C). When the coals are ready, nestle the wood chunks among them and fill the reservoir with water. Place the meat loaf in the center of the lower cooking rack. (Replenish the charcoal, adding one third the number you started with each 30 minutes of cooking.)

2. Cook for 60 minutes, until the meat loaf has shrunk away from the sides of the loaf pan. Then lay a length of foil across the top of the pan. Using hot mitts, place the palm of one hand on top of the foil while the other hand grips the bottom of the pan. Gently turn the meat loaf over onto the foil in your palm. Keeping the loaf on the foil, place it back on the cooking rack (do not fold the foil over the meat) and continue smoke cooking another 60 minutes.

3. Remove the meat loaf carefully from the smoker, let sit 10 minutes, then cut into thick slices to serve hot, or chill for great hunting day sandwiches.

Melt-in-Your-Mouth Smoked Meat Loaf

ROASTS

The Elementary Roast

Any four-legged animal yields two kinds of roasts: tender ones and tough ones. Tender roasts are best cooked hot and dry, while tougher roasts are best cooked moist and slow. That holds true whether you are talking commercial or wild—elk, whitetail, moose, or mammoth. What also holds true for all four-legged meat animals is that the most tender cuts come from the upper rear quarter; move down the leg or up the spine and the meat will be tougher. But tougher, especially when you are talking wild meat, is a relative term. I've had old bulls that are tough from the tenderloin on down, and forkhorn whitetail stew meat that you could cut with a fork. The best thing is to test a small (2 ounce/50 g) shoulder steak as soon after you get the animal home as possible (see page 10 for the shoulder steak test). If that shoulder steak is tender enough to cut with a table knife, the whole animal will fall into the tender meat category, and you can cook any of it any way you want to.

The other thing to remember with roasts is that it is the thickness of the cut, not the total weight, that determines cooking time. A long, slender, 2-pound (1-kg) tenderloin will cook faster than a squarish 2-pound rump; thus a whitetail rump will cook faster than an elk rump even though they bear the exact same name. The most common error with roasts is overcooking. Because it is low in fat, venison is always best cooked rare or medium—not well done. Personally, I prefer my beef that way too, even though beef's higher fat content gives you more of a margin of error. That margin is critical in venison. Just a few degrees over medium and all cuts become tougher and drier.

The most predictable way of judging the internal temperature of a roast is with a meat thermometer. Use an ordinary $3.95 meat thermometer, but remember that the roast's temperature will rise 5–10 degrees after it is removed from the cooker—and the last 30 degrees of cooking occurs very quickly. Divide the estimated cooking time in half, insert the meat thermometer, check it, then depending on how close the roast is to being done, check again in 5, 10, or 15 minutes. Those last 30 de-

grees can take 7–10 minutes, depending on your barbecue. Use the traditional readings for beef to keep track of your venison: rare is 130° F (54° C) and medium is 140° F (60° C), so if you want rare, remove the roast at 120° F (49° C).

As for the cooker? They are all different. Charcoal kettle barbecues with a vented hood and bowl are the easiest to control; propane barbecues are made to operate in overdrive. Generally speaking, you can hold your hand at cooking level for 3 seconds over a very hot fire; 4–5 seconds over a medium-hot fire; 6–7 seconds over a medium to low fire. Since different people have different tolerances, try an oven thermometer to be sure: the hot setting on my propane barbecue is about 600° F (315° C) at the cooking surface; moderate heat is about 400° F (205° C). The lowest setting I can get is 250° F (120° C), and that's with the barbecue on low and the tank choked down. For most quick grilling, the 4–5 second range is ideal.

As you can see from these temperatures, there is absolutely no reason why you cannot cook a venison roast in the barbecue. No reason, even, why you have to always cook them over indirect heat or on a rotisserie. All you have to do is preheat the propane or start the charcoal, trim and pat dry the roast, and season it. Then before the cooking rack gets hot, oil it to prevent sticking. Once the grill is preheated, start the roast. Start it frozen, as in the No-Brainer Frozen Whitetail Roast (see recipe on page 47), or at 400° F (204° C), as I do with the Bourbon Rump (see recipe on page 50) to sear in the juices. After 20–30 minutes, turn the roast, bottom to top, and stick a meat thermometer into the thickest part, without touching bone. Monitor it every 10 minutes after that, until you learn how fast your fire cooks in your barbecue. For serving, slice the finished roast thick or thin, but always cut across the grain for tenderness.

I've included thickness as well as weight with the first few roasts to show how those dimensions affect cooking time. But remember that an undercooked roast is easily fixed. Err on the side of rare.

RAPID ROY THE TENDERLOIN

Yield: 2–3 servings

Here's the quickest roast that was ever cooked—outside of a microwave. And for an intense condiment, make the sun-dried tomato dipping sauce.

Rapid Roy the Tenderloin

Ingredients

1 cup (250 ml) sun-dried tomatoes
½ cup (125 ml) hot water
3 cloves garlic, minced
1 tablespoon plus 1 teaspoon vegetable oil
1 tablespoon balsamic vinegar
1 cup (250 ml) beef bouillon
½ teaspoon salt
½ teaspoon pepper
1 pound (½ kg) antelope or deer tenderloin
    (1½ inches/3¾ cm thick)

Preparation

Put the tomatoes in a small bowl and cover them with hot water to soften, about 15–20 minutes. When the tomatoes are soft, dice them up. In a medium-hot skillet, sauté the garlic in 1 tablespoon of the oil until lightly browned, then add the diced tomatoes. Sauté about 2–3 minutes, then add the vinegar, bouillon, salt, and pepper and sauté another 3–4 minutes until the sauce is hot again. Transfer to a food processor or blender and purée. Set aside.

Cooking

1. Preheat a propane barbecue for 10 minutes, then turn it down to medium high heat. Or start 40 charcoal briquettes, wait 25 minutes, and, when you cannot hold your hand at cooking level for more than 4–5 seconds, the fire is ready.

2. Trim the roast, and pat it dry with paper towels. Lightly brush or wipe the roast with oil, and place it directly over the coals. Close the lid on the barbecue and cook 10 minutes. Turn the roast over, and cook another 10 minutes until the second side is nicely seared. Continue cooking, about 25 minutes in all, and turning when one side starts to get a little overdone. Test the roast with a meat thermometer after the first 15 minutes, then remove it when the meat thermometer reads 130° F (54° C) for rare or 140° F (60° C) for medium. Don't start a game of Monopoly; this roast will cook in less than half an hour. Slice thick and serve on a deli roll with a generous dollop of the sun-dried tomato sauce, which can be either hot or chilled.

BONNEVILLE TENDERLOIN

Yield: 4 servings

Unless you are extremely unlucky, the tenderloin and the back straps—both of which run on both sides of the spine, the former outside the rib cage, the latter inside the body cavity between the rib cage and hip—are always going to be very tender and very tasty. A quick, dry roasting is perfect for such a delicacy, and this salt runway not only adds a tangy flavor, but also keeps the bottom of the roast from getting crisped.

Preparing the salt flat for the Bonneville Tenderloin.

Ingredients
2 cups coarse kosher salt
½ cup (125 ml) water
2 pound (1 kg) moose or elk tenderloin
   (about 2 ½ inches/6 ½ cm thick)
1 teaspoon pepper
2 teaspoons dried leaf basil

Cooking
1. Preheat a propane barbecue for 10 minutes and turn the heat down to high. Or start 4 dozen charcoal briquettes and wait 25 minutes. When you cannot hold your hand at cooking level for more than 5–6 seconds, start cooking.
2. In the meantime, combine the salt and water in a medium-sized bowl. It will form a loose paste. Transfer the salt paste to a length of aluminum foil longer than the loin, and press the paste into a thin brick that is ¼ inch (½ cm) thick and 9 inches (23 cm) long.
3. When the barbecue is ready, lay the brick and aluminum liner on the cooking rack, then gently place the loin on the brick. Season the roast with the pepper and basil, close the lid, and cook about 10 minutes to sear in the juices. Then turn the temperature down (or adjust the coals and vents) to a medium setting (about 400° F/205° C). Test the roast with a meat thermometer after another 20 minutes, and cook until the thermometer registers 130° F (54° C) for rare to 140° F (60° C) for medium done. (Total cooking time will be about 40–45 minutes.) Serve with grilled corn on the cob and folded fettuccine tossed with butter and grated Parmesan cheese to taste.

No-Brainer Frozen Whitetail Roast

Yield: 6–8 servings

If your house is like our house, you have a freezer full of wonderful meat and never have anything thawed for dinner. Well, worry no more. If you have a meat thermometer and an hour to relax, dinner is on the way.

With low-fat venison, the most tender and flavorful meat is rare and medium done. Cook it to well done, and you may as well be eating hockey pucks.

Ingredients
2½ pound (1¼ kg) boned and rolled rump roast (2½ inches/6¼ cm thick)
2 tablespoons hot sweet mustard
1 tablespoon Worcestershire sauce

Cooking
1. Preheat a propane barbecue 10 minutes then turn down to medium; or start 4 dozen charcoal briquettes and wait 25 minutes until the coals are white hot.
2. Meanwhile, unwrap the roast from the freezer paper, and microwave it for 6 minutes at 500 watts (4 minutes at 700 watts) until just a half inch of the roast is thawed. (That's so you can get the meat thermometer started into the center.)
3. In a small bowl, combine the mustard and Worcestershire sauce, stir well, and wipe this mixture over the roast. Insert the meat thermometer, then place the roast in the preheated barbecue, about 4 inches (10 cm) above the heat, and close the lid.
4. Check the progress in 30 minutes. When you get to about 120° F (49° C) on the meat thermometer, the temperature will rise very quickly. Those last 10–20 degrees go at a rate of 2–4 degrees per minute.
5. In about 45 minutes, total, the roast should be at 130°–140° F (54°–60° C), or rare to medium rare in the center. At that temperature you will have a roast with something for everyone: medium on the outside and rare in the very middle. Slice thin and serve with mashed potatoes.

THE LARDED BUCK

Yield: 4–6 servings

This is the roast for those who like the juices running down their arms. Larding is an age-old method of adding fat—and flavor—to meat. It involves a bit of work, which you can do 24 hours ahead of time if you want, but the flavor is well worth the trouble.

Ingredients

3 tablespoons chopped green onion
1 tablespoon dry sherry
1 teaspoon soy sauce
½ teaspoon sugar
½ teaspoon ground ginger
½ teaspoon white pepper
3 pound (1½ kg) mature buck roast (about 3½ inches/9 cm thick)
2 slices bacon
½ teaspoon black pepper

Preparation

1. In a small bowl, combine the green onion, sherry, soy sauce, sugar, ginger, and white pepper, and stir to mix. Trim all fat and sinew from the roast, and pat dry with paper towels. Cut each slice of bacon into 3-inch (7½-cm) lengths and slice each length into ¼-inch (½-cm) strips.

2. With a very sharp, pointed knife, poke slits into the top of the roast, straight down with the blade, ½ inch (1¼ cm) short of punching through the bottom. Carefully, slide some of the seasoning mixture into the slit, backed by a strip of bacon. Continue making slits across the top of the roast at about 1-inch (2½-cm) intervals, until almost all of the bacon and seasoning are used up. Wipe the last of the sauce over the roast, then lay 2–3 pieces of bacon on top and sprinkle with the black pepper.

Cooking

1. Preheat a propane barbecue for 10 minutes, then turn down to medium heat. Or start 40 charcoal briquettes, wait 25 minutes, then divide the coals in half and place around a drip pan. When you can't hold your hand over the fire for more than 4–5 seconds at cooking level, start cooking.

2. Brush a little oil on the bottom of the roast, or on the cool rack to prevent sticking. Then place the roast on the cooking rack above the drip pan, close the lid, and cook about 45 minutes for rare, 50 for medium. On the meat thermometer, inserted into the thickest part of the roast, that's 130° F (54° C) for rare, 140° F (60° C) for medium. Let the roast sit 5–10 minutes before carving. Serve with succotash and sweet potatoes.

Mule deer buck and doe. (Photograph © Mark & Jennifer Miller Photos)

CHERRY-SMOKED ANTELOPE ROAST WITH CRANBERRY—SOUR CREAM SAUCE

Yield: 6–8 servings

If you've tried hickory smoking and the much lauded mesquite, it's about time you gave fruitwood a try. Fruitwood has a milder, mellower sweet flavor that's not overly sweet. Hard to describe. Try it—you just might find something new to put under your cranberry sauce on holidays.

Cherry-Smoked Antelope Roast with Cranberry–Sour Cream Sauce

Ingredients

¼ cup (60 ml) cranberry sauce
1 teaspoon sour cream
1 teaspoon dried mint leaves
1 cup cherry wood chips
4 pound (2 kg) rump roast (3½ inches/9 cm thick)

Preparation

Liquefy the cranberry sauce in a medium-sized bowl in the microwave or in a double boiler. While the sauce is still hot, add the sour cream and stir it in until it is completely dissolved. Add the mint leaves and set aside. Place the wood chips in water and let them soak for 15–30 minutes.

Cooking

1. Preheat a propane barbecue for 10 minutes, then turn down to medium high heat. Or start 40 briquettes and wait 25 minutes. When the coals are so hot you cannot hold your hand at cooking level for more than 4–5 seconds, the fire is ready.

2. Trim the roast and dry it with paper towels. Wipe or brush a small amount of oil on the roast and bring it out to the barbecue with the wood chips. For charcoal, strew the chips on top of the hot coals; for propane, fill a smoke box with the chips and nestle it among the fake coals on one side of the grill.

3. Set the roast on the cooking rack and cook about 10 minutes; turn the roast over and cook another 10 minutes to brown both sides. After the first 20 minutes, remove the roast to the upper shelf, or away from the fire, and continue cooking until a meat thermometer reads 130° F (54° C) for rare, 140° F (60° C) for medium. (About 40 minutes total cooking time.)

4. Remove the roast from the barbecue and let it sit 5–10 minutes before slicing, while you reheat the sauce in the microwave or double boiler. Slice thin and serve with the cranberry–sour cream sauce.

BOURBON RUMP

Yield: 4 servings

I did an informal survey a couple of years ago among my closest friends, asking what item of food they would not be able to do without on a 5-day camping trip. The women listed chocolate, cookies, candy—everything with sugar and fat. The men listed beer or liquor first, then loaded up on condiments to make their meat taste good: tabasco, steak sauce, ketchup, and soy or teriyaki sauce. So this is a man's recipe—the men might have to borrow the molasses from the women's tent.

Ingredients

3 tablespoons bourbon whiskey
⅓ cup (80 ml) ketchup
2 tablespoons molasses
2 tablespoons soy sauce
2 tablespoons olive or canola oil
¼ teaspoon freshly ground black pepper
½ cup (125 ml) lager beer
3 pound (1½ kg) rump roast (or other tender roast)

Preparation

In a medium-sized saucepan, combine the bourbon, ketchup, molasses, soy sauce, oil, pepper, and beer. Bring to a low boil, then lower the heat to a simmer and cook, stirring occasionally, for about 5 minutes. Let the bourbon mixture cool to room temperature.

Cooking

1. Preheat the propane barbecue for 10 minutes, then turn down to medium high heat. Or start 40 charcoal briquettes and wait 25 minutes, until you cannot hold you hand over the coals for more than 4–5 seconds.

2. Place the rump on a lightly oiled cooking rack, close the lid, and cook on medium high (directly over the coals in charcoal cooking) for about 5 minutes. Then brush the meat liberally with the bourbon sauce, close the grill, turn the heat down to medium (for charcoal, move the roast from directly above the coals) and cook another 30–40 minutes. Check for doneness with a meat thermometer: 130° F (54° C) for rare, 140° F (60° C) for medium. The initial high heat seals in the juices, while the moderate heat prevents the bottom of the roast from getting overcooked. Serve with grilled acorn squash.

Antelope buck in belly-high grass.

BUTTERFLIED LEG OF VEAL

Yield: 6–8 servings

The principle of butterflying is to take a thick piece of meat and create more surface area for sauces, and for that delicious barbecue-grilled finish. It is also faster to cook than a big roast, and unlike a pile of steaks, is easier to handle. Last but not least, butterflied meat can be a dramatic centerpiece for a different sort of holiday feast.

Ingredients

5 pound (2½ kg) veal leg
¼ cup (60 ml) minced fresh thyme leaves
1 tablespoon ground lemon peel
⅓ cup (80 ml) minced fresh cilantro
1 teaspoon pepper
¼ cup (60 ml) vegetable oil
3 sturdy metal skewers

Preparation: 3–24 hours ahead

1. Butterflying the veal leg: Begin with one thigh bone—rump roast and round steaks still in one piece but boned off of the hip bone and with the lower leg separated. Remove the femur by making a straight cut down through the meat, the entire length of the bone. Fillet the meat from the bone and lift it out.

2. Now you need to even the playing field. Press the boned meat out as flat as you can, then make one long cut down (but not completely through) the thickest part on each side; flatten that, and make 2 or 3 more long cuts, as needed, until you can press the meat out to a relatively consistent 2- or 3-inch (5–7½-cm) thickness. (Be careful not to cut through the meat as you work. You want it to be all one piece.) Pat the leg down with paper towels to dry.

3. Combine the thyme, lemon rind, cilantro, pepper, and oil in a bowl, and rub this semidry marinade onto all sides of the meat, especially into the cuts. Place the veal leg in a shallow baking dish, cover, and refrigerate for 2–24 hours.

Cooking

1. By indirect cooking: Preheat your propane barbecue for 10 minutes, then turn down to medium heat. Or start 4 dozen charcoal briquettes and wait 25 minutes. For charcoal, place a drip pan in the center of the grill and arrange the hot coals on both sides. In a propane unit, place a drip pan on the unlit side of the barbecue (or, if you have two shelves, on the lower one).

2. Lift the meat from the marinade and let the juices fall back into the pan. Lay the leg on a flat surface and thread one skewer through the longest, thickest part of the butterflied leg (about 2 inches/5 cm in from the edge); thread a second skewer along the other long side of the leg, at an angle so it crosses the first one. Add a third skewer if you wish, across the first two to stabilize the leg for turning.

3. Place the butterflied leg on a lightly oiled rack and cook about 45 minutes, brushing with the marinade until it is gone and the meat thermometer inserted in the thickest part reads 130° F (54° C) for rare, 135° F (57° C) for medium rare. Because the butterflied leg has many different thicknesses it will have rare, medium and medium well portions for the table when done. Slice thick or thin and serve with tabbouleh salad and sourdough bread brushed with vegetable oil and toasted on the dying coals.

RIBCAGE AND JERKY

MARINATED AND GRILLED WHITETAIL HEART

Yield: 2 servings

My husband, John, is a heart connoisseur. His favorite recipe used to be parboiled and fried, but this is a summer recipe to warm the cockles.

Ingredients
1 whitetail heart
⅛ cup (185 ml) red wine vinegar
¼ cup (60 ml) oil
3 cloves garlic, chopped
2 teaspoons ground cumin
1 teaspoon red pepper flakes
1 teaspoon chili powder
2 medium-sized tomatoes, minced
½ cup (125 ml) chopped onion
1 canned jalapeño pepper, minced
1 tablespoon fresh lime juice
2 teaspoons minced fresh cilantro
¼ cup (60 ml) sour cream (or nonfat yogurt)
2 sweet potatoes, cooked fork tender
1–2 tablespoons vegetable oil

Preparation
1. Rinse the heart in cold water as soon as possible after the kill. Trim off all fat and connective tissue and cut into 1-inch (2½-cm) chunks. Pat dry. Combine the wine vinegar, oil, garlic, cumin, red pepper flakes, and chili powder in a bowl and add the heart cubes. Cover and refrigerate overnight.
2. Combine the tomatoes, onion, jalapeño, lime juice, cilantro, and sour cream in a small bowl. Cover and refrigerate overnight.

Cooking
1. Preheat a propane barbecue for 10 minutes, then turn down to high to cook. Or start 4 dozen charcoal briquettes and wait 25 minutes. If you are using wooden skewers, soak them in water for 20–30 minutes. The fire is ready when you cannot keep your hand at the cooking level for more than 4–5 seconds.
2. Meanwhile, remove the meat cubes from the marinade, dry them, and throw away the marinade. Cut the sweet potatoes into 1-inch (2½-cm) cubes. Thread the skewers alternately with the cubes of meat and sweet potato. Spray or brush the oil on the meat and potatoes, and place the skewers on the grill. Cook until the outside of the food is browned and crisp, 4–5 minutes to a side. Serve dipped in the sour cream salsa.

Whitetail buck in the mist. (Photograph © Michael H. Francis)

MR. CHOLESTEROL RIBS

Yield: 4–6 servings

Here's proof that there are ways to make a healthy, low-cholesterol wild elk as fat as a pig. The best part is you can parboil the ribs and make the sauce ahead of time, then have a quick dinner whenever you are ready. But use a drip pan to prevent fat flare-ups.

Mr. Cholesterol Ribs

Ingredients
4 pounds (2 kg) elk ribs
6 tablespoons bacon drippings
6 tablespoons butter
½ medium onion, chopped fine
½ cup (125 ml) cider vinegar
2 tablespoons Worcestershire sauce
½ teaspoon salt
1 teaspoon pepper

Preparation
1. Trim the outer fat from the ribs, and put in a large pot with enough water to cover. Bring to a boil, then lower the heat and simmer 25–30 minutes until most of the fat is rendered.
2. While the ribs parboil, make the sauce. In a medium-sized saucepan, melt the bacon drippings and butter over medium heat, then add the onion, vinegar, Worcestershire sauce, salt,

and pepper. Raise the heat until the mixture comes to a light boil, then lower the heat and simmer 10–15 minutes, until the sauce is a shiny liquid. Set aside until you are ready to cook.

Cooking
1. Start 4 dozen briquettes, or preheat a propane barbecue and turn down to high heat. When the charcoals are white hot and you can only hold your hand at cooking level for 3–4 seconds, place a drip pan under the cooking surface. Dip the ribs in the barbecue sauce and place them on the grill.
2. Starting with the meaty side down, barbecue hot, 7 minutes on each side. Wipe with more sauce when you turn the ribs, then again just before you take them off the grill. Serve with baked beans.

EASY BACON DRIPPINGS

Save your drippings next time you cook bacon, or try this: place 3–4 slices of bacon in a microwave-safe dish. Cover to prevent splattering, and microwave 1–3 minutes, pouring off drippings until you have enough. Make a BLT with the cooked bacon and save the drippings for the ribs.

A bull moose—one of the best candidates for rib and brisket recipes. (Photograph © Michael H. Francis)

LAZY-DAY RIBS

Yield: 4–6 servings

I have never understood why marinades take 8–12 hours. You either end up putting it together, or eating it, at breakfast. A 24-hour marinade is much more civilized. Prepare it while your kids wash the dishes, or while the dishwasher washes them, if your kids have all flown, and let it sit till dinnertime the next day.

Ingredients
3–4 pounds (1½–2 kg) deer ribs
12 ounces (360 ml) pale ale
½ medium onion
⅓ cup (80 ml) bottled chili sauce
¼ teaspoon garlic powder

Preparation
Trim all outer fat off the ribs. In a blender, combine the pale ale, onion, chili sauce, and garlic powder and purée. Pour into a resealable plastic bag, and add the trimmed ribs. Seal and refrigerate 24 hours.

Cooking
1. Preheat your propane barbecue, one burner only, then turn down to low, 220°–250° F (105°–120° C). Or start 30 charcoal briquettes; in 25 minutes, when the coals are ashy, spread the coals out in a single layer. You should have the same temperature as above. If you need to cool the fire a bit, spread the coals apart, raise the cooking rack, or shut the bottom vents halfway. To heat it up, do the opposite.
2. Pour the ribs and sauce into a 9x13-inch (22x32-cm) disposable aluminum pan, cover with aluminum foil and seal. Carefully place the pan on the cooking rack and close the barbecue lid. Cook 2–2½ hours, until the rib meat is falling off the bones. Serve with rice.

WHAT MAKES GOOD RIBS?

1. The bigger the animal, the meatier the ribs. Deer and antelope will work; moose and elk are superb.
2. Use ribs from sweet-tasting (not gamy) animals only. It is impossible to remove all the fat from ribs, which is why we like them, but if an animal is gamy, those bad flavors are concentrated in the gristle, fat, and sinew. Cook a round steak or some stew first. If that tastes good, then you can cook the ribs with confidence.
3. Trim all exterior fat well. (Or parboil the ribs, as in the Mr. Cholesterol Ribs recipe, if you need to be ruthless.) Venison fat is a lot more like mutton tallow—even on good animals—than it is like beef and pork fat. And the fat of bighorn sheep tastes exactly like mutton fat. But parboiled even bighorns make good ribs.
4. Tough animals can make good ribs, but use an oven bag or aluminum foil packet to cook them as tender as possible.

Kahlúa Ewe Ribs in a Bag

Yield: 4–6 servings

A ewe bighorn sheep, or young ram—not in the rut—makes a lamblike rib dish. I like my ribs nearly falling off the bone, so I decided to try out an oven bag to tenderize them. It works even better than the foil packet, but you do need to be careful not to let the barbecue rise much above 350° F (177° C) while cooking. That's why I did it in the propane barbecue. You can cook the Kahlúa Ewe Ribs just as deliciously with charcoal, but keep a close eye.

Bighorn sheep at rest. (Photograph © George Robbins Photo)

Ingredients
3–4 pounds (1 ½ –2 kg) bighorn sheep ribs
½ cup (125 ml) vodka
½ cup (125 ml) Kahlúa
½ teaspoon ground anise seed
¼ teaspoon ground cloves

Preparation
Trim off all outer fat, then parboil 20–30 minutes to render the rest of the fat. (This is very important with sheep, even if the meat tastes delicious. Remember, wild sheep, genetically, is very closely related to mutton.) In a resealable plastic bag, combine the vodka, Kahlúa, anise, and cloves, shake gently till dissolved and add the ribs. Seal and refrigerate 24 hours.

Cooking
1. Preheat your propane barbecue, one burner only, then turn the heat down to low, 220°–250° F (105°–120° C). Or start 30 charcoal briquettes; in 25 minutes, when the coals are ashy, spread them out in a single layer. You should have the same temperature as above. If you need to cool the fire a little bit, spread the coals apart, raise the cooking rack, or shut the bottom vents halfway. To heat it up, do the opposite.

2. Prepare a large plastic oven bag per package directions, making sure to dust the inside with flour, and poke several slits in the top. Transfer the ribs and marinade into the bag, seal shut with the enclosed ties, and place in a barbecue-safe baking pan.

3. Place the pan of ribs and sauce in your barbecue, cover, and cook at low temperature for 2–2 ½ hours, until the rib meat is falling off the bones. Serve with mashed potatoes and pan juices.

KANSAS CITY–STYLE BARBECUED ELK RIBS

Yield: 6–8 servings

Let your ribs sit in the rub for 24 hours, or lightly rub and sit only 1 hour—the difference is in the intensity of flavor. Buttered-noodle types be warned: This is elk with an attitude.

Kansas City–Style Barbecued Elk Ribs

Ingredients
6 pounds (3 kg) elk ribs
3 chunks of hickory

Rub
1 cup (250 ml) brown sugar
½ cup (125 ml) sweet Hungarian paprika
1 tablespoon black pepper
1 tablespoon white pepper
1 tablespoon salt
1 tablespoon ground cumin
1 tablespoon chili powder
1 tablespoon onion powder
1 teaspoon crushed red pepper flakes

Sauce
¼ cup (60 ml) water
4 teaspoons vegetable oil
1 cup (250 ml) tomato paste
2 tablespoons plus 2 teaspoons molasses
½ cup (125 ml) white vinegar
2 teaspoons prepared horseradish
1 teaspoon ground allspice
½ cup (125 ml) minced onion
¼ teaspoon garlic powder
1 ½ teaspoons salt
1 ½ teaspoons pepper

Preparation
1. Trim the exterior fat from the ribs and pat dry with paper towels. Place the hickory chunks in a bucket of water. Soak 2–3 hours. In the meantime, combine the rub ingredients in a shallow bowl. For spicy ribs: apply about one third of the rub mix to the ribs, then place the ribs in a resealable plastic bag and let sit in the refrigerator 24 hours. For mellower ribs, but still tangy: apply the rub lightly, then set in the refrigerator 1 hour.
2. While the rub works, prepare the sauce. Combine all the sauce ingredients in a blender, purée, and refrigerate.

Cooking
1. In a water smoker, at 240°–250° F (115°–120° C): Drain the wood chunks and place them among the coals, or around the electric element. Fill the water basin and preheat the cooker.
2. When the cooker is ready, place the ribs on the cooking racks, and close the lid. Cook 2–2 ½ hours, mopping the ribs with sauce in the last half hour, and at the table only. Serve with a three-bean salad.

LOW-FAT CAROLINA ELK BRISKET

Yield: 8–10 servings

This is barbecue, Carolina-style. Instead of a sweet, heavy Texas- or Kansas City–style sauce, the meat is cooked with a tangy vinegar baste. It's one of those regional variations we are losing. Blame it on TV, homogenized milk, and McDonald's. We're all starting to eat too much alike.

Ingredients
4 pounds (2 kg) elk brisket
2 teaspoons salt
3 teaspoons black pepper
1 cup (250 ml) apple cider vinegar
2 teaspoons red pepper Tabasco sauce
2 teaspoons sugar

Preparation
1. Trim the fat from the brisket and dry with paper towels. Combine 1 teaspoon of the salt and one teaspoon of the pepper, and rub it into the meat. Set aside.
2. In a small bowl, combine the cider vinegar, Tabasco sauce, sugar, and the rest of the salt and pepper. Stir well until the solids dissolve.

Cooking
1. In a 22-inch (54-cm) covered grill, start 30 charcoal briquettes. In 25–30 minutes, when the coals are ashy, place a drip pan the size of the brisket in the center of the barbecue. Divide the coals in half and mound them on two sides of the drip pan. Now, check your heat.

Hold you hand at cooking level: low heat will allow you 7 seconds over the coals (200°–220° F/95°–105° C). To cool the fire, spread the coals apart, raise the cooking rack, or shut the bottom vents halfway.
2. Pour 1 inch (2½ cm) of water into the drip pan, and lightly spray or rub the cooking rack with oil. (Always remove the rack from the fire before applying oil.) Place the brisket over the drip pan, brush lightly with the sauce, and cover the grill. Cook for 2–2½ hours, brushing with the sauce every 30 minutes. Also every 30 minutes replenish the coals and the water as needed. (To replenish coals, add a third more new coals to the hot fire, evenly distributed—with 30 coals, add 5 more to a side each 30 minutes till the last 45–60 minutes of cooking.) Do not turn the brisket.
3. To serve, slice thin and pile high on deli rolls with cherry butter (red currant jelly is close). Or, for a tangier flavor, serve the traditional way: Shred the meat into a large bowl and toss with the pan juices.

*Bull elk.
(Photograph ©
George Robbins
Photo)*

TIPSY BRISKET

Yield: 2½ pounds (1¾ kg)

Brisket is about the toughest chunk of meat on any animal, coming off the outside of the upper rib cage. Because of the toughness, it is traditionally used for the long soak of corned venison and the slow cooking of real barbecue. An elk-sized animal, or larger, has a good-sized brisket; deer-sized animals have a smaller brisket that I usually leave for the ribs (since deer also have less meat on their ribs). Deer brisket will work in a pinch.

Tipsy Brisket

Ingredients
4 hickory wood chunks
2–3 pound (1–1½ kg) elk brisket
2 teaspoons salt
1 teaspoon pepper
¾ teaspoon ground ginger

Sauce
⅓ cup (80 ml) Madeira
1 tablespoon Worcestershire sauce
2 tablespoons vegetable oil
1 tablespoon red wine vinegar
½ teaspoon dry mustard
1 tablespoon brown sugar
2 teaspoons onion powder

Preparation
1. Two hours before you want to start cooking, cover the wood chunks with water and let soak.
2. Trim the fat from the brisket and dry with paper towels. Combine the salt, pepper, and ginger in a small bowl and rub the seasoning mix over the surface of the meat.
3. Combine the sauce ingredients in a small bowl and set aside.

4. Preheat your propane barbecue, one burner only, then turn down to low. Now, check your heat: hold your hand at cooking level. Low heat (about 250° F/120° C) will allow you 7 seconds over the coals. (If your propane unit isn't that cool at low, try turning the propane tank itself down. But be careful to keep the fire from flickering. A light wind could blow out the flame. Or, cook with charcoal, as in the Low-Fat Carolina Elk Brisket [see recipe on page 59].)

Cooking
1. Drain the wood chunks, then place directly on the "coals." While the cooking rack is off, lightly spray or rub it with oil to prevent sticking, and place a pan with 1 inch (2½ cm) of water on the lower rack.
2. Place the brisket over the drip pan and brush with the sauce. Cover and cook for 2–2½ hours, until the meat is very tender, brushing with the sauce each half hour. Do not turn the brisket.
3. To serve, slice thin across the grain, and drizzle the remaining cooking sauce over the top.

MESQUITE-SMOKED TWELVE-HOUR FAJITA JERKY

Makes 6 ounces (150 g) jerky

This is the safest and easiest way to make smoked jerky. Fire up the old smoker, set it at a constant 140° F (60° C) and at the end of the day, you have delicious jerky. I've known people who turn a whole elk into jerky, even the back straps, and others who make duck and goose breast into jerky, as well. I prefer to use tough cuts only, but any of the above will do.

Ingredients
2 pounds (1 kg) red meat, duck, or goose breast
$\frac{1}{3}$ cup (80 ml) sugar
2 tablespoons salt
1 cup (250 ml) red wine
1 medium onion, quartered
4 cloves garlic
1 whole canned jalapeño pepper
$\frac{1}{2}$ teaspoon cinnamon
$\frac{1}{4}$ teaspoon dried leaf oregano
$\frac{1}{8}$ teaspoon ground cloves
$\frac{1}{4}$ cup (60 ml) sour cream
3 cups (750 ml) mesquite chips

Mesquite-Smoked Twelve-Hour Fajita Jerky

Preparation
1. Trim all fat and sinew off the meat, then slice thinly ($\frac{1}{4}$–$\frac{1}{8}$ inch/$\frac{1}{2}$–1 cm thick) with the grain. It's easiest to do this when the meat is about three-quarter frozen. Place the sliced meat in a noncorrosive bowl or a resealable plastic bag.
2. In a blender or food processor, combine the sugar, salt, wine, onion, garlic, jalapeño pepper, cinnamon, oregano, cloves, and sour cream. Purée, and pour over the meat slices. Stir or shake to coat the meat. Refrigerate, covered or sealed, 12–24 hours.

Cooking
1. Remove the meat from the marinade without rinsing and allow to air dry on paper towels for 1 hour. While the meat dries, put the mesquite chips in a bowl of water and let them soak at least 15 minutes.
2. Place the meat on the racks in your smoker, and turn it on. Use 1 cup (250 ml) of mesquite chips per hour in the first 3 hours of smoking. Then leave the smoker alone for another 8–9 hours. When done, the jerky will be dry to the touch but still pliable, not brittle.
3. Place the jerky in a jelly bag, or small bag made from game bag fabric, and let it hang in a cool dry place, free of bugs, for another 48 hours to make sure all the moisture is gone. Once dry, store in the refrigerator or freezer in sealed glass jars, resealable plastic bags, or vacuum sealed bags.

TWO-HOUR CHEATIN' HICKORY JERKY

Yield: 3 ounces (75 g) jerky

If you've ever had the urge to make jerky but didn't have all day or didn't want the oven on 8–12 hours in the middle of August, look to your barbecue. If you are very good at fire control and can keep the barbecue's temperature down to a consistent 220°–240° F (105°–115° C) you can cook jerky in only 2 hours. Otherwise, cook it in the little aluminum smoker.

*Two-Hour
Cheatin' Hickory
Jerky*

Ingredients

1 pound ($\frac{1}{2}$ kg) trimmed steaks, partially frozen

$\frac{1}{2}$ cup (125 ml) Worcestershire sauce

$\frac{1}{2}$ cup (125 ml) soy sauce

$\frac{1}{2}$ cup (125 ml) V-8 juice

$\frac{1}{4}$ cup (60 ml) brown sugar

$\frac{1}{2}$ teaspoon concentrated liquid hickory smoke

$\frac{1}{2}$ teaspoon onion powder

$\frac{1}{4}$ teaspoon garlic powder

$\frac{1}{4}$ teaspoon pepper

Preparation

1. About 90 minutes before you plan to start cooking, remove the steaks from the freezer and defrost very briefly, just enough to slice very thin pieces off the steaks. (Frozen steaks, to a point, are much easier to slice than mostly thawed ones.)

2. In a shallow bowl or baking dish, combine the Worcestershire sauce, soy sauce, V-8, brown sugar, liquid smoke, onion powder, garlic powder, and pepper. Stir until the solids have dissolved, then add the thinly sliced steak. Cover and marinate in refrigerator for 1 hour only.

Cooking

1. Drain the marinade off the steak slices, and let them sit at room temperature 15 minutes. Meanwhile, start the propane barbecue and turn it down immediately to the lowest setting. Choke down the tank valve, too, until you have a constant 240° F (115° C). For charcoal, start 30–35 briquettes on one side of the barbecue, wait 25 minutes, then spread them out a bit on that side. You should be able to hold your hand at cooking level for 6–7 seconds, again at 240° F (115° C).

2. Spread some aluminum foil out on the rack in the coolest part of the barbecue, then spread the meat on the foil, making sure the pieces don't touch. Cook about 60 minutes, until the meat turns very dark—almost black—and looks dry. Fold the ends of the foil over the top loosely, then cook one more hour until the meat is well dried. Remove the meat from the cooker and let it cool before eating. Place the jerky in a plastic bag and refrigerate any leftovers. They will keep up to 2 weeks.

Season your ground meat, then partially freeze on cookie sheets lined with wax paper. This is one of the easiest ways I've found to slice easy-chewing burger jerky into uniform pieces.

PERFECT JERKY

Jerky should be cooked at a low temperature until all the moisture is out of the meat. That does not mean the meat should be dry, brittle, and unappetizing. Think of it as Walter Mathau's face: it should be dry and wrinkled, but still quite mobile. And to keep it from falling apart while you are slow cooking it, jerky should always be cut with the grain. (Roasts and steaks, for tenderness, are cut across the grain.)

THE BEST CUT: KEEPING KNIVES SHARP

Whether you are trimming ribs, slicing jerky extra thin, or just trimming brisket for the smoker, diamond stones, ceramic sticks, steels, and Arkansas stones will make the job faster and easier.

A few passes now and then, in the midst of a big job, will keep your knife sharper longer.

UPLAND BIRD RECIPES

To me, upland birds are a warm weather walk through steep alder patches, or a sweaty trek across broken field into creek willows. The bird-hunting season actually lasts into December, but, I admit, most years I get way-laid by big game. Then after the deer and elk season is over, I'm so tired I can't even think about another frigid afternoon in the field. So bird hunting gets short shrift.

Enter Druzilla, the strawberry-yellow Labrador. Dru's the newest addition to our family, turning one year old this year right in the middle of big game season, about one week after my husband broke his foot. So ask me how much big game hunting I did this year. One day. I was lone shooter for our rookie bird dog. There were the usual blue and ruffed grouse in the September alder and pheasants among the golden autumn cottonwoods, but then there were the Hungarian partridge in the wheat stubble, ducks on the one or two back channels of the Missouri River that hadn't frozen over yet, and the odd sharptail grouse hanging out midst the silvery leaves of a buffalo berry patch. I discovered that the warmth of a game bird in my vest could be quite wel-come on a cold December afternoon. Then came the plucking, plucking, and more plucking.

It reminded me of some basic rules: there are two good times to pluck birds. First, when the bird is still warm. (But there are more birds to shoot then.) The sec-ond best time is about a week later. If the bird was shot in hot weather, you need to draw it out and put it on ice as soon as possible (within 1–2 hours). If the thermom-eter is down to jacket weather you can handle the bird more leisurely. Of course for transporting it home in a heated vehicle, drawn or whole, put it on ice.

Once home, place the bird, whole, in a plastic bag in the bottom of the refrigerator for 5–7 days. Then the feathers will come easily. If you need to wrap and freeze the bird before this, you are best off skinning rather than plucking. And if you are hunting land that has been farmed—with herbicides, pesticides, anhydrous ammonia, and the rest—it's best to skin most or all of your upland birds anyway. If the birds live among those chemicals, they will be stored in the fat—and filtered through the liver. While we do not eat livers, be careful to keep your bird dog from scarfing up any entrails as a snack in the field. You may end up with a big vet bill.

After you've cooled your game birds in the field and aged them in the refrigerator, double wrap them for the freezer and you will eat birds all year. Take a deep breath, and the next thought will be, "What's the best way to cook all these wonderful creatures?" Unless you are in-credibly unlucky, 70–90 percent of the birds you shot are young of the year. Cooking methods depend on the bird involved. Mountain grouse tend to be tender all over; other birds tender in the breast, tougher in the leg. Young pheasant (you can tell they're young if the beak bends and the spur is rounded) are less tough in the leg than sage or sharptail grouse—birds that make their living in the Big Open. Sharptail and sage grouse also are among the most "distinctly" flavored, and can be improved with an overnight milk bath if that flavor offends. Tough birds, or tough legs, can be water-smoked or cooked in an oven bag and made quite tender, or ground and turned into sausage. And, yes you can use a plastic oven bag in the barbecue. Just be sure you don't cook much hotter than 350° F (175° C).

Here are some very specific ideas for that bulging freezer.

Page 65: A drumming ruffed grouse. (Photograph © Michael H. Francis)

How To Cut Up a Bird

There are lots of ways to serve birds. Some birds like geese and turkeys are almost always served whole. Ducks, pheasants, Hungarian partridge, and other smaller birds are served up whole some of the time, but more often are parted out. Whichever your choice, here is the method I use to part out upland birds. (To cut up waterfowl, see "The (Almost) Boneless Duck" on page 85. You can also adapt the method below to waterfowl by skipping the wishbone section in Step 6. Waterfowl wishbones are much too stout to clip.)

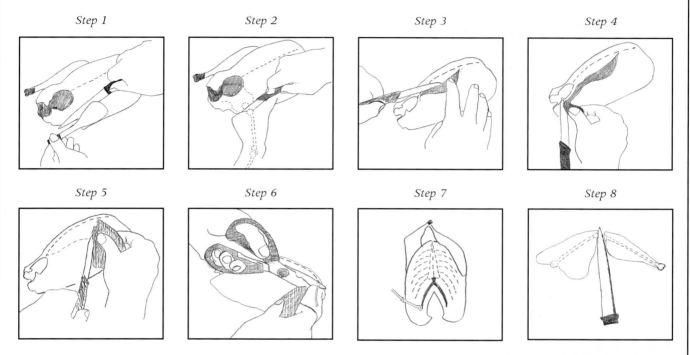

Step 1 | *Step 2* | *Step 3* | *Step 4*

Step 5 | *Step 6* | *Step 7* | *Step 8*

Step 1: To divide a bird into legs and breast, start with the legs. With the bird on its back, hold the end of one leg out from the body. Cut through the skin between leg and carcass, keeping the knife vertical and as close to the carcass as you can. Most of the meat here is on the thigh, so cutting close to the carcass will cut down on loss of leg meat.

Step 2: Once you've cut through the skin, stretch the leg out to the side, and feel your way down to the hip joint where the ball-end of the femur (upper leg bone) fits into the socket opening of the hip. Cut through the connective tissue and cut the leg free.

Step 3: With the leg separated from the carcass, you can now cleanly cut the breast free of the sternum and rib cage. Lay the bird on its back, and feel for the top of the sternum (dotted line in drawing), running down the center of the breast. Starting mid-sternum, run your knife down one side of the sternum, separating the meat from the bone.

Step 4: You should be able to see the bony-white of the sternum now (dotted outline). With your knife, scrape the breast meat from mid-sternum down to the belly opening. Lift the flap at the end of the breast.

Step 5: Now scrape the breast meat from the sides of the rib cage, working forward to the neck opening. For ducks and geese, whose wishbones are much thicker than upland birds, go ahead and free the meat from the rib cage. For upland birds, stop when you reach the wishbone. There's a simple trick to get a few more bites of delicious white meat off of each breast.

Step 6: Clip through the top of the wishbone, as shown in the drawing. Then scrape the rest of the breast meat free of the rib cage and sternum, until the only place it is still connected is at the bottom of the wishbone. Here, the upper wing bone (or humerus) joins with the scapula (or shoulder blade) and clavicle (also known as the collar bone in humans but when fused together in bird skeletons, called the wishbone) to form the shoulder joint.

Step 7: In this front view, you can see how the clavicle and wing come together at the shoulder. Slice through the tendons and ligaments at the shoulder joint and free the breast. Repeat steps 1–6 for the other side.

Step 8: To divide the thigh from the drumstick: hyperextend the knee joint (bend it the opposite way it's meant to bend) to loosen and stretch the ligaments. Then slice those ligaments between the thigh bone (femur) and lower leg bones (fibula and tibia).

CHILI MOUNTAIN GROUSE

Yield: 4 servings

*Blue grouse.
(Photograph ©
William H.
Mullins)*

Mountain grouse are blessed by nature to live in a low aerobic environment. Fortunate for the grouse, doubly fortunate for the cook. They are very easy to handle: legs are tender; flesh is white and mild most of the season. (For spruce grouse, limit this recipe to early season birds. In the late season, they take to eating conifer needles and their meat can be bitter.)

Ingredients

2 mountain grouse
Juice of 2 limes
1 clove garlic
2 tablespoons olive oil
5 dashes red pepper Tabasco sauce
½ teaspoon salt
½ teaspoon pepper
6 sprigs fresh oregano (5 inches/10 cm each)

Preparation

1. Split the grouse in half by cutting with a poultry shears up one side of the spine and up the sternum (the breastbone). At the top of the sternum, you will need to turn the bird over and snap the breastbone out. (You may also want to lift the ribs from the meat.) Then flatten the boned breast and trim any sharp edges. Dry with paper towels and set aside.
2. In a blender or food processor, combine the lime juice, garlic, oil, Tabasco, salt, and pepper and purée. Pour the juice over the split birds and let marinate no more than 30 minutes.

Cooking

1. Preheat a propane barbecue for 10 minutes and turn down to medium high. Or start 40 charcoal briquettes and wait 25 minutes. The fire is ready when you cannot hold your hand at cooking level more than 4–5 seconds.
2. Drain the birds and discard the marinade. Place oregano sprigs on the hot coals and the split birds on the grill. Cook about 4–5 minutes a side. Serve on a bed of couscous; add salsa if desired.

HEAVENLY BLUES WITH CRISPY POTATOES

Yield: 2 servings

This is one of my favorite summer meals. The grouse is light and fresh tasting and the crispy potatoes fill the belly. Fix it at the end of August, when you start thinking how miserable it will be to chase grouse up and down the alder patches on hot September days. Somehow it always motivates me.

Heavenly Blues with Crispy Potatoes

Ingredients
4 tablespoons olive oil

$\frac{1}{4}$ cup (60 ml) freshly squeezed lemon juice (1 lemon)

4 large garlic cloves, peeled

4 bay leaves

2 teaspoons grated fresh lemon peel

Breasts of 2 blue grouse

Crispy Potatoes
2 medium potatoes

2 teaspoons vegetable oil

2 tablespoons grated Parmesan cheese

$\frac{1}{4}$ teaspoon black pepper

Preparation
1. Combine the olive oil, lemon juice, garlic, bay leaves, and lemon peel in a blender and purée until the bay leaves are well minced. Pour the marinade into a resealable plastic bag or medium-sized bowl and add the grouse. Seal or cover and refrigerate 1–2 hours.

2. Precook the potatoes whole in a microwave, 4 minutes at 700 watts (6 minutes at 500 watts). Cool.

Cooking
1. Preheat a propane barbecue for 10 minutes and turn the heat down to medium high. Or start 40 briquettes and wait 25 minutes. The fire is ready when you cannot hold your hand at cooking level for more than 4–5 seconds.

2. While the barbecue heats up, prepare the potatoes. Chunk them into 1-inch ($2\frac{1}{2}$-cm) pieces. Toss in a plastic bag or bowl with the vegetable oil, Parmesan cheese, and pepper. Place in a hinged grate and cook over the fire 15 minutes, turning often.

3. Drain the birds from the marinade and discard the marinade. When the potatoes are about halfway done, place the birds on the grill and cook about 4 minutes a side. When done, there will be no pink in the thickest part of the cut. To serve, arrange the crispy potatoes around the grouse.

WHAT KNOTS

Yield: 4 servings

What Knots can be made with pheasant as I've done here, or with any bird you have in your freezer. Sweet and tangy in flavor, they also have the fat we all crave when we've been out all morning in a cold stand. Serve them after the hunt, or as appetizers at your next game feast. But beware—they are addictive.

What Knots

Ingredients
1 pheasant, cut into 1-inch (2½-cm) cubes
4 slices bacon, halved lengthwise
¼ cup (60 ml) soy sauce
1 tablespoon brown sugar

Preparation
Wrap each pheasant cube in a length of bacon and secure on a wooden skewer. You can line up 3 or more knots to a skewer, but be careful that all the knots on one skewer are the same thickness. In a shallow dish, combine the soy sauce and brown sugar and brush each knot with the mixture several times over the next 20 minutes.

Cooking
1. Meanwhile, start the barbecue. Preheat a propane barbecue for 10 minutes, then turn the heat down to medium high. Or start 40 charcoal briquettes, wait 25 minutes, and when you can't hold your hand at cooking level more than 4–5 seconds your fire is ready.
2. Place each skewer on the grill and cook about 4–5 minutes a side, watching out for fat fires. Remove from the grill when the bacon is browned, and serve as appetizers.

QUICK RASPBERRY PHEASANT

Yield: 4 servings

Start the marinade 48 hours ahead, then when you're ready to cook, drain the birds and convert the marinade into a tangy, at-the-table meat sauce. This is a recipe for young birds only. Test the beak to see if it bends, and the spurs to make sure they are not sharp.

Quick Raspberry Pheasant

Ingredients
½ cup (125 ml) oil
¾ cup (185 ml) raspberry vinegar
1 teaspoon poppy seeds
3 teaspoons sugar
2 pheasants
¼ teaspoon salt
2 tablespoons sour cream

Preparation
In a resealable plastic bag, combine the oil, vinegar, poppy seeds, and sugar and mix. Part out the birds: legs and breasts. Dry them off with paper towels and place them in the bag with the marinade. Refrigerate, sealed, for 48 hours.

Cooking
1. Preheat a propane barbecue for 10 minutes and turn down to medium high. Or start 40 charcoal briquettes and wait 25 minutes. When the fire is ready, you should only be able to hold your hand at cooking level for 4–5 seconds.

2. Meanwhile, drain the marinade into a saucepan. Bring the sauce to a boil, then turn the heat down and simmer for 5 minutes. Turn the heat off and stir in the sour cream. Keep warm.

3. Pat the pheasant part dry with paper towels and season with the salt. Place the legs on the grill, and cook for 10 minutes, turning 2–3 times. Add the breasts to the rack, and cook both legs and breasts another 6–8 minutes, turning once halfway through this final cooking. The meat will be just done: opaque white for the breast, and a rich brown—but not bloody—for the legs.

4. Serve on a bed of rice, with the raspberry sauce spooned over the top.

MESQUITE-SMOKED PHEASANT TACOS

Yield: 4 servings

Two ways to do the smoke: Make a hot fire with chunks of mesquite, or make a fire with charcoal briquettes and add a generous handful of mesquite chips to the coals just before cooking. But since we're cooking this up fast, use only the breast. Save the legs for White Sausage (see recipe on page 117).

Ingredients

Breasts of 2 pheasants
1 teaspoon ground cumin
1 teaspoon chili powder
½ teaspoon salt
½ teaspoon pepper
8 corn tortillas
1 tablespoon vegetable oil
4 Roma tomatoes, diced
2 cups (500 ml) sliced lettuce
4 ounces (100 g) Monterey Jack cheese, grated
1 cup (250 ml) red salsa

Preparation

Dry the breasts with paper towels and set aside. In a small bowl combine the cumin, chili powder, salt, and pepper and stir to mix thoroughly. Rub this mixture on both sides of the breasts, cover, and place in the refrigerator 30–60 minutes.

Cooking

1. Preheat a propane barbecue for 10 minutes, then turn down to medium high heat. Or start 40 charcoal briquettes (or mesquite chunks) and wait 25 minutes. The fire is ready when you cannot hold your hand at cooking level more than 4–5 seconds. If you are using mesquite chips over the charcoal, set them to soak for 15–20 minutes while the fire is getting hot.

2. Brush the tortillas with a small amount of oil. Prepare the tomatoes, lettuce, cheese, and salsa.

3. Place the breasts on a lightly oiled grill directly over the fire and cook about 4–5 minutes to a side. As the pheasant cooks, lightly brown the tortillas over the fire, about 2–3 minutes each. Stack on a serving platter and cover to keep soft. When the pheasant is done, remove it from the fire and tear or slice the meat apart.

4. Divide the pheasant, tomato, lettuce, cheese, and salsa among the tortillas, fold, and eat.

PHEASANT IN THE BAG

Yield: 2 servings

Summer or winter, there are always tough birds in the freezer, and you can't cook tough birds quickly over a hot fire. So if the beak doesn't bend and the spurs are sharp, try slow cooking with a little moisture.

Late season rooster pheasant. (Photograph © John Barsness)

Ingredients

1 tablespoon flour
¾ cup (185 ml) dry white wine
1 teaspoon dried thyme leaves
¼ teaspoon cinnamon
¼ teaspoon black pepper
1 pheasant, whole
1 apple, cored and sliced
1 onion, sliced

Cooking

1. Preheat the propane barbecue for 10 minutes, then turn down to medium low (about 350° F/175° C). Or start about 3 dozen charcoal briquettes on one side of the barbecue, and wait 25 minutes. Test for the same heat with an oven thermometer.

2. In a plastic oven bag, combine the flour, wine, thyme, cinnamon, and pepper and mix. Dry the pheasant off with paper towels, insert the apple and onion slices inside the body cavity, and seal the bird in the bag. Place on a clean aluminum drip pan.

3. Place the pan with the prepared bird in the barbecue, away from direct heat and cook 60 minutes. (In a 2-burner propane unit, place the pan on the unlit burner, or on a shelf above the lit one. On charcoal, keep the coals on one side of the grill, and place the bird on the other.)

4. Remove the bird from the bag and let it cool 5–10 minutes. Separate into serving pieces and serve with the oven bag juices.

CREAMED PHEASANT WITH CARAMELIZED ONIONS

Yield: 4 servings

No matter what else I cook, this is what people remember. It harkens back to the classic pheasant fried in butter, then baked in cream sauce, but this is a lot easier. With the caramelized onions, I think it tastes a lot better, too.

Ingredients

2 tablespoons butter
½ onion, thinly sliced
¼ cup (60 ml) extra dry sherry
½ cup (125 ml) heavy cream
2 tablespoons Dijon mustard
¼ teaspoon white pepper
1 pheasant, cleaned
1 tablespoon flour

Cooking

1. In a large skillet, melt the butter over medium heat, then add the onion slices and sauté until the onions are golden brown—caramelized. Turn the heat off and let the onions sit.
2. Preheat a propane barbecue for 10 minutes, then turn down to medium low heat. Or start 3 dozen charcoal briquettes on one side of the barbecue and wait 25 minutes. Optimum cooking temperature is 350° F (175° C) for both units.
3. While the barbecue heats up, combine the sherry, cream, mustard, and pepper in a small bowl. Mix thoroughly. Pat the pheasant down inside and out with paper towels and set it in a plastic oven bag that has been shaken with 1 tablespoon of flour. Pour the cream sauce and caramelized onions over the pheasant and close the bag. Make 6 small slits in the top of the bag, per package directions. Now place it on a clean drip pan for easy handling.
4. Place the pheasant in the barbecue, on the top shelf or over the unlit burner, and cook 60 minutes. Remove the pheasant from the bag, and serve with the cream sauce and mashed potatoes.

GOLDEN PHEASANT

Yield: 2 servings

Because of the water in water smoking, you can smoke a 1½-year-old pheasant and still be able to eat the legs. You also end up with a beautiful, mahogany-colored main course.

Ingredients
4 chunks hickory wood
1 orange, whole, peeled
1 pheasant, skin on
Vegetable oil

Preparation
Two hours before you want to start cooking, set the wood chunks in a bucket of water. Drain before using.

Cooking
1. In an electric water smoker, place the drained chunks of hickory on the coals, then fill the water reservoir and plug in. For a charcoal water smoker, start the coals, following the manufacturer's directions for achieving a cooking temperature of 220°–240° F (105°–115° C), then once you reach 240° F fill the water reservoir and place the drained chunks of hickory on the coals through the coal door.

2. Stuff the orange inside the pheasant, then rub oil on the outside of the bird. Spray or rub oil lightly on the grill.

3. Place the pheasant over the center of the water reservoir, then close the lid. Cook 2–2¼ hours. Remove the orange before serving. Serve hot as a main course with sweet potato salad, or chill and serve as an appetizer.

The one that got away. (Photograph © William H. Mullins)

PORTLY PRAIRIE GROUSE

Yield: 4 servings

Port makes a robust sauce for this distinctly flavored denizen of the sagebrush. If you don't have sage or sharptail grouse near you, a handful of quail, or a quartet of Hungarian partridge will stand up to the task.

Ingredients

2 sharptail grouse, cleaned
2 cups (500 ml) milk
2 tablespoons butter
1 cup (250 ml) dry red wine
1 cup (250 ml) ruby port
½ cup (125 ml) water
½ teaspoon chicken bouillon granules
3 cloves garlic, minced
3 tablespoons apple juice concentrate
1 teaspoon salt
½ teaspoon pepper

Sharp-tailed grouse. (Photograph © Michael H. Francis)

Preparation

About 8–24 hours ahead of time: Split the grouse in half with a poultry shears by cutting up along one side of the spine in back. For the front, turn the bird breast down. Then, while pressing on each shoulder joint, snap the breastbone out. Finish by cutting neatly through the breast meat. (You will have 2 equal halves; ½ breast and 1 leg to each.) Place the 4 split sides in a shallow bowl and cover with milk. (If you like very strong-tasting birds, don't bother with the milk bath.)

Cooking

1. Preheat a propane barbecue for 10 minutes, then turn it down to medium high heat. Or start 40 charcoal briquettes and wait 25 minutes. The fire is ready when you cannot hold your hand at cooking level more than 4–5 seconds.

2. Drain the milk off the split birds, and dry them with paper towel. Set them aside. In a large skillet, melt the butter and add the wine, port, water, bouillon granules, garlic, and apple juice. Bring the sauce mixture to a boil, then turn the heat down to low and simmer until it thickens. (When ready it will stick to the spoon.) Keep the sauce warm while you cook the birds.

3. Season the grouse with salt and pepper inside and out, and place on a lightly oiled cooking rack directly over the heat. Cook about 5 minutes a side for rare, 6–7 for medium. Serve with green tomatoes, sliced, breaded, and fried.

SMOTHERED QUAIL WITH BLACK WALNUT SAUCE

Yield: 4 servings

California quail. (Photograph © William H. Mullins)

When I first saw California in the 1960s, I fell in love with all the walnut trees and dreamed of having wild walnuts in my yard. Here's the closest I've come: wild quail butting up against store-bought walnuts.

Ingredients

½ cup (125 ml) chopped walnut meats
¾ cup (185 ml) vegetable oil
½ cup (125 ml) dried bread crumbs
4 teaspoons red wine vinegar
2 teaspoons balsamic vinegar
¼ teaspoon red pepper Tabasco sauce
¼ teaspoon salt
4 whole quail

Cooking

1. Preheat a propane barbecue for 10 minutes and turn down to medium low. Or start 3 dozen charcoal briquettes and wait 25 minutes. The cooking temperature should be about 350° F (175° C).
2. In a blender or food processor, combine the walnuts, oil, bread crumbs, vinegars, Tabasco sauce, and salt, and purée.
3. Pat the quail down with paper towels, and place on a piece of aluminum foil large enough to wrap all four birds. Spoon the sauce over the birds and seal up the foil.
4. Place the packet in the barbecue and cook 45–50 minutes, until the legs come when you pull at them. When done, transfer packet contents to plate. Serve with garlic toast and fresh green salad.

SUCCULENT SMOKED SAGE GROUSE

Yield: 4 servings

The secret to good sage grouse, as with any strong bird, is to shoot young birds, gut and rinse them quickly, and cool them fast. Failing that, or sometimes even with that, an overnight milk bath followed by a slow, wet cooking is not only your best bet, but also a delicious remedy for one of Nature's crueler tricks. (How could she make such a magnificent looking bird taste so much like a telephone pole?)

Male sage grouse in display. (Photograph © William H. Mullins)

Ingredients
2 sage grouse, whole
1 quart (1 liter) milk
3 chunks cherry wood
3 cups (750 ml) red wine
1 tablespoon dried leaf oregano
1 orange, sliced

Preparation
1. Dry the grouse with paper towels and place in a resealable plastic bag with the milk. Let the birds soak overnight. Drain the milk.
2. Set the wood chunks to soak in a pail of water, about 2 hours.

Cooking
1. Set up your water smoker: Drain the wood chunks and place on the coals (fake or charcoal). Fill the reservoir with the wine, oregano, sliced orange, and enough water to reach 2 inches (5 cm) from the top of the bowl. Plug in the electric smoker, or light the charcoal. The unit should cook at 240° F (115° C).
2. When the cooker starts to smoke, place the birds on the cooking racks, and close the lid. Cook 2½–3 hours. Let them sit 10 minutes to cool, then slice the birds and serve with grilled carrots and corn on the cob, or chill the birds, and serve sliced thin for an appetizer.

CHRISTMAS IN JULY TURKEY

Yield: 8–10 servings

Sometimes it doesn't seem like there are enough holidays for turkey, so it's time for July to take some heat. Outdoors, that is, in the barbecue—where a wild bird belongs. By the way, this bird is also stuffed, but to make the recipe easy, the stuffing is not cooked before placing it in the bird.

Male Merriam turkey. (Photograph © William H. Mullins)

Ingredients

4 cups (1 liter) dried bread cubes
¾ cup (185 ml) milk
1 cup (250 ml) butter, melted
2 eggs, lightly beaten
2 stalks celery, diced
½ cup (125 ml) chopped green pepper
¾ cup (185 ml) chopped onion
1 cup (250 ml) chopped almonds
½ teaspoon salt
½ teaspoon pepper
8–10 pound (4–5 kg) turkey
3 tablespoons mayonnaise

Cooking

1. Preheat a propane barbecue for 10 minutes, then turn down to medium low heat (about 350° F/175° C). Place a drip pan on the fake coals. Or start 4 dozen briquettes, wait 25 minutes and mound the coals on two sides of the drip pan (again, 350° F/175° C).
2. While the barbecue preheats, soak the bread cubes in the milk for about 10 minutes. Meanwhile, stir the butter and eggs together in a large bowl, then add the celery, green pepper, onion, almonds, salt, and pepper. Gently fold in the milky bread. Dry the turkey with paper towels, and fill the bird lightly with the stuffing mixture just before you start cooking.
3. Place the bird over the drip pan, wipe the mayonnaise over the breast, legs, and wings and insert a meat thermometer into the thickest part of the breast. Close the barbecue. Allow 15 minutes per pound of bird, replenishing coals at the rate of about 8 per side, per hour, starting when you begin cooking.
4. The bird is done when the meat thermometer registers about 140° F (60° C) for medium, 150° F (66° C) for medium well. Unless you shot your turkey on a game farm, or prefer your birds dry, I recommend not cooking the turkey to the traditional 170°–180° F (77°–82° C) marked on most meat thermometers. Those temperatures are for birds raised in overcrowded, unhealthy conditions.
5. Remove the stuffing right away and let the bird sit 10 minutes before carving. Serve with fresh garden and potato salads.

ALDER-SMOKED TURKEY SALAD

Yield: 4–6 servings

I know how it is. You have family or company coming and the thermometer is somewhere up in the upper 90s. Who wants to cook? Sounds like a classic day for an electric water smoker, cooking outdoors, without any help at all from the troops. And if you want something special for a game dinner or holiday buffet, forget the salad part of the recipe: just smoke the turkey. Check the catalogs: a 12 pound (6 kg) alder-smoked turkey sells for $54. Most wild adult gobblers dress out at about 12 pounds (6 kg), so you get the picture.

Ingredients

4–5 chunks alder wood
1 whole turkey, cleaned (10–15 pounds/5–7 kg)
2 tablespoons apple jelly
½ pound (¼ kg) Swiss cheese, cubed
3 red delicious apples, peeled, cored, and cubed
1½ cups (375 ml) walnut meats, quartered
1 tablespoon prepared Dijon mustard

4 tablespoons red wine vinegar
1 teaspoon sugar
1 teaspoon salt
½ teaspoon black pepper
1 tablespoon chopped green onions (greens only)
¼ cup (60 ml) olive or canola oil

Preparation

1. Cover the alder wood chunks with water and let them soak 2–3 hours.
2. Drain the wood chunks and place them carefully among the fake coals of the water smoker. Fill the water reservoir, and plug in the cooker to preheat for 10 minutes. While you wait, pat the turkey dry with paper towels, and liquefy the apple jelly in the microwave (about 2 minutes at 500 watts; 1 minute at 700 watts). Brush or rub the liquid jelly over the turkey, then place it breast up on the upper rack of your smoker and close it up.
3. Smoke the turkey 3 hours, then remove it from the smoker and let it cool down to room temperature.

Making the salad

1. Once the turkey has cooled, cube up at least 1½ pounds (¾ kg) of the meat, both breast and leg meat. Cubes should be about ½ inch (1 cm) thick. Combine the cubed turkey with the cheese, apple, and walnuts; gently toss. Transfer to a salad bowl or to individual plates.
2. In a small bowl, combine the mustard, vinegar, sugar, salt, pepper, green onion, and oil. Stir until well mixed and the oil turns slightly thick. Drizzle the dressing over the salad. Serve with fresh sourdough bread.

Male Rio Grande turkey in full strut. (Photograph © Michael H. Francis)

WATERFOWL RECIPES

The Elementary Duck

Personally, I prefer mallards, but I know lots of people who think mallards have about half as much flavor as ducks were meant to have. Either way, they're still a lot more trouble to eat, per pound, than venison. Oh, sure, it's a lot easier to drag any duck out of the field than any elk, but what about plucking? Before I knew how to do it the easy way, I spent 3 hours dry plucking a duck. And yes, there is an easy way.

Start with dry plucking, like with upland birds. The easiest time to dry pluck a duck is when it first lands in the blind. Second best is a week later, after it has aged in your refrigerator or hung in your garage at 35°–45° F (1–7° C). That duck I spent 3 hours pulling feathers from? It had aged only 2 days, which is about the worst possible time to try to pull feathers. Do it right away or wait a week.

If you simply can't wait, or have a lot of birds to take care of, wet plucking will make the job go faster. Half fill a large soup or canning pot with water and bring it to just under a boil, then add 1 teaspoon liquid dishwashing detergent. Dip the ducks in the water one at a time or, if you have a wide pot, two or three at a time. Turn them gently in the water for about 15 seconds. Haul them out and wait until each bird is cool enough to handle or until the breast feathers pull easily. Then pluck the duck. What you can't pull can be singed with a candle or propane torch, gently.

Wet plucking or dry plucking, it's easier to do with a whole duck, head and guts intact. Once you've aged and plucked the bird, make a slit up the belly and draw the entrails out. Cut the head off at the shoulders and reach into the neck cavity to finish removing the esophagus and any other viscera lurking in the chest. Rinse, and pat the bird dry, then double wrap it in plastic wrap and foil, or plastic wrap and freezer paper. The freezer paper allows for a longer freezer life, but, because of their fat, waterfowl are best eaten within 6–9 months no matter how good the wrap job.

So after you have plucked a whole Christmas goose, a whole New Year's mallard, a whole goldeneye, and a whole teal for each birthday, there's an even easier way to care for your waterfowl. Breast and leg them. The legs are perfect for sausage, and the breasts can be skinned, or left with the skin on. Many people who hunt lots of waterfowl save time and energy with this method.

Cooking the bird is more complex. You can cook the breast, or a whole or halved duck, quickly over a hot grill. This direct method of cooking waterfowl requires constant vigilance to prevent fat flare-ups from charring the bird. Whole geese should be cooked indirectly, by lighting the typical 4 dozen briquettes, but then banking them around a drip pan and letting the bird cook over the drip pan. This not only keeps the bird moist and the skin from scorching, but also keeps the fat from falling directly into the fire, thus leaving the water pistol in the drawer and the griller at ease. Cooking time varies with the method: time a 1-inch-thick (2½-cm-thick) breast or half duck as you would a 1-inch-thick (2½-cm-thick) steak. On a hot fire, 5–6 minutes to a side. Thinner cuts take less time. Whole geese should cook on a moderate fire (350° F/175° C) for about 12–15 minutes a pound until a meat thermometer registers 160°–180° F (71–82° C) medium to well. (Generally, unstuffed birds take 12–13 minutes per pound, stuffed birds 15 minutes per pound.) My propane barbecue, on a medium low setting, is about 350° F (175° C), but since whole birds take a long time cooking, slight variations in temperature can cause large variations in total cooking time. You should check your barbecue with an oven thermometer.

Which brings us to the issue of rare birds. Read any cookbook, except one that really knows wild birds, and it will recommend cooking a bird to an internal temperature of 170°–180° F (77°–82° C). That's for domestic birds; birds that are raised in close quarters. If you are cooking wild birds that never lived in cages or pens, and which have not been concentrated in such numbers that they suffer the same illnesses as caged birds, you don't have to cook your dinner to a crisp. Do keep track of reports from your state's fish and game department of epidemics among wild birds. And do continue to cook your game-farm, pen-raised, and put-and-shoot birds to 170°–180° F (77°–82° C). But if you have a wild bird, born and lived wild, you can enjoy it cooked to a quite rare or medium rare (130°–140° F/54°–60° C) finish. Use a meat thermometer inserted in the thickest part of the breast to be sure the bird is exactly the way you want it.

Page 81: Pintails over the marsh. (Photograph © Bill Marchel)

Mallard drakes. (Photograph © Jeffrey Rich Nature Photography)

TIPS ON SAFELY THAWING MEAT

Since we all live and die by what's in the freezer, here's something to think about. Whether you are talking domestic or wild, birds or venison, never thaw any meat at room temperature. You should always thaw meat in the refrigerator: allow 24 hours for each 5 pounds of bird, which usually is as much as a wild goose will weigh. If you need to speed up the process, microwave large cuts 1–2 minutes at a time, checking frequently, until the bird feels slightly warm to the touch. Then transfer it to the refrigerator until it is ready to cook.

Tried duck recipes from conventional cookbooks? Here's why they don't work. The adult wild mallard on the left weighs about a third of the commercial duckling at right. Mainstream cookbooks design recipes around the commercially raised bird, not the smaller, older, less fatty, and often less tender wild bird we collect during hunting season. You can convert recipes back and forth; just take the differing size, fat, tenderness, and age into account.

Common goldeneye. (Photograph © Jeffrey Rich Nature Photography)

THE (ALMOST) BONELESS DUCK

Because the wishbone and sternum are so stout in ducks, people mainly end up cooking the birds whole, or slicing the 2 halves of the breast off the sternum, ending up with two smaller portions—especially if the duck in question is a teal rather than a big northern mallard. There is a way to keep the breast whole, however, and to have a large, juicy bird to serve for special occasions. It takes a bit more effort, but you end up with an entire bird with only 12 bones. And those 12 are large—consisting exclusively of the upper and lower leg bones. (I've also used this method in pheasants, to have a larger breast at the table.) Here's how it's done.

Step 1

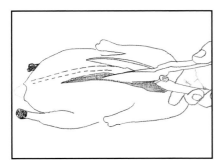

Step 2

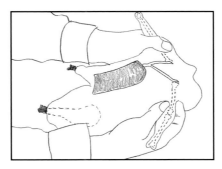

Step 3

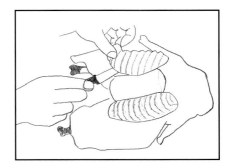

Step 4

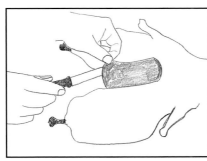

Step 5

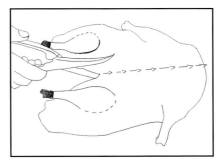

Step 1: Begin by removing the backbone (dotted line in drawing). Lay the bird on its breast and, with a sharp pair of poultry shears, slice up one side of the spine, keeping as close to the spine as possible. Repeat for the other side of the spine. Lift the spine out.

Step 2: With the bird still breast down, pick it up by the shoulders, placing the thumb of each hand over the upper wing bone (humerus) and the rest of your hand under it. With a quick snap of the wrist, hyperextend the shoulder, pressing both upper wing bones at the same time (see upper hand in drawing for placement; lower hand is to the side to illustrate the bone structure), until your knuckles meet behind the bird. This will pop the shoulder joint apart, and, in small and young ducks and in most upland birds, will pop the sternum (breastbone) out of the meat.

Step 3: With a paring knife, lift the loosened rib cage intact from the carcass. At this point the meat is fairly well

separated from the rib cage. Repeat with second rib cage.

Step 4: Now lift the loosened sternum. With some birds, this will require very little help with a knife; in others, you'll need to lift the bone and fillet the meat. To clean up the last of the bones, fillet the wishbone and hip bone out. The hip bone will be loose from having cut out the spine in Step 1. Run your fingers over the meat to be sure you've picked up all the bones.

Step 5: The (almost) boned bird can now be laid out on the grill whole (or split, as shown) and cooked at moderate temperatures. Or, if you like lots of stuffing, it can be stuffed and tied with white cotton string, then slowly roasted in the grill, as for a whole goose (allow 20 minutes per pound at 350° F/175° C). For hot, quick grilling, remove the legs and cook them separately: they will not cook as fast as the breast. With or without legs, this is an elegant way to serve fowl. At the table, slice across the breast.

QUICK-AND-DIRTY DUCK ON THE VINE

Yield: 2 servings

Heat up the grill and keep your water pistol handy—we're going to hot grill a duck.

Quick-and-Dirty Duck on the Vine

Ingredients
1 ½ pound (¾ kg) duck, cleaned
½ cup mango flavored vinegar
1 cup grapevine chips
½ teaspoon garlic salt

Preparation
1. Split the duck in half with a pair of poultry shears by cutting through the ribs up one side of the spine, then turn the bird over and cut up through the sternum (the breastbone) until you reach the top. Put the shears down and take one side of the breast in one hand and the other in your other hand, body cavity toward you, and snap the top of the sternum. Trim any sharp edges with the shears, and rinse the duck thoroughly. Dry it off with paper towels.
2. Place both halves in a shallow baking dish, and pour the mango vinegar over the top. Cover and set in the refrigerator for 30–60 minutes. While the duck marinates, set the vine chips to soak in water for 30 minutes.

Cooking
1. While the vines and the duck soak, start up the barbecue. Preheat a propane barbecue for 10 minutes, then turn down to medium high for cooking. Or start 40 charcoal briquettes, wait 25 minutes, and when you cannot keep your hand at cooking level for more than 4–5 seconds, the fire is ready. You want the fire as hot as you would need it for searing steaks. Now fill your water pistol or squirt bottle with water.
2. Drain the chips and strew them among the charcoals, or place them in a wood box nestled among the fake coals for a propane barbecue. Place the duck halves on the grill, skin side up, and sprinkle the garlic salt on them. Cover the barbecue and cook 7–10 minutes, until the undersides are nicely browned, then turn the duck halves over, and let the skin side get browned as well. Finish cooking the ducks on the top rack. Put out fat fires as necessary.
3. The duck is done when a meat thermometer inserted in the meatiest part of the breast registers 130° F (54° C) for rare, 140° F (60° C) for medium, about 25 minutes total. Serve sliced, with wild rice, or eat the duck with your fingers.

The V-notch in the tail means a young and tender duck.

GRILLED DUCK STRIPS WITH SPICY RASPBERRY SAUCE

Yield: 4 servings

I wish shooting ducks were as easy as making this versatile and delicious recipe. Serve these kabobs up as appetizers or design an entire dinner around them. Either way, be sure to keep your strips at least 1 inch (2 $\frac{1}{2}$ cm) thick—just the right size to keep the meat moist, but make the cooking quick.

Ingredients
$\frac{1}{2}$ cup (125 ml) raspberry preserves
$\frac{1}{2}$ cup (125 ml) diced green onion
4 teaspoons apple cider vinegar
4 teaspoons soy sauce
1 teaspoon garlic powder
1 teaspoon salt
Breasts of 4 mallards

Preparation
At least 24 hours ahead, combine the preserves, onion, vinegar, soy sauce, garlic powder, and salt in a bowl. Mix well, cover, and refrigerate.

Cooking
1. If you are using wooden skewers, place them in water to soak for 30 minutes. Then start the fire. For propane, preheat the grill on high for 10 minutes, and turn down to medium high heat. For charcoal briquettes, start 40 briquettes and wait 25 minutes. The fire is ready when you cannot hold your hand at cooking level for more than 4–5 seconds.

2. While the grill heats up, slice the duck breasts into 1-inch-wide (2 $\frac{1}{2}$ -cm-wide) strips and thread onto the skewers. Place the skewers on a lightly oiled cooking rack, and cook the duck until medium rare, about 3–4 minutes a side, turning often. Serve hot, dipped in chilled raspberry sauce.

BoBo Brake's Fabulous Blind Duck

Yield: 4 servings

My friend Tom says he actually hunted in a blind that came equipped with a barbecue. The guide kept a resealable plastic bag in his pocket with this marinade, and as the clients killed ducks, he breasted, marinated, and cooked them on the spot. I'd say Tom's got a tough life. But there's no beating this marinade for truly fresh ducks.

Ingredients

A mallard drake. (Photograph © William H. Mullins)

¾ cup (185 ml) soy sauce
1 teaspoon ground ginger
¼ teaspoon garlic powder
¼ cup (60 ml) vegetable oil
Breasts of 2 mallards, skinned

Preparation

1. Combine the soy sauce, ginger, garlic powder, and oil in a resealable plastic bag. Take it for a ride; shoot up some steel.
2. Breast out the duck, and dry each serving off with paper towels. Place them in the marinade for 30 minutes.

Cooking

1. In the meantime, start your barbecue. Preheat a propane barbecue for 10 minutes, then turn down to medium high. Or start 40 charcoal briquettes, wait 25 minutes, and when you cannot keep your hand at cooking level for more than 4–5 seconds, the fire is ready.
2. Drain the breasts from the marinade, pat dry, and place on the hot grill. Cook about 4 minutes a side for rare mallards; 5–6 for medium. Slice thin, and serve as an appetizer or for fortification in a cold and snowy duck blind.

GLAZED DUCK LEGS

Yield: 2–3 servings

So you breasted all those mallards and now you have a bag of legs in the freezer that, by law, you must keep, but, by heavens, you don't know how to make tender. Well, relax. That's what water smokers were invented for.

Ingredients
½ cup (125 ml) hoisin sauce (a Chinese condiment)
2 tablespoons orange marmalade
2 tablespoons soy sauce
¼ teaspoon crushed red pepper flakes
12 mallard (or other) duck legs

Cooking
1. In a small bowl, combine the hoisin sauce, marmalade, soy sauce, and red pepper flakes. Brush or wipe the sauce on the duck legs. Set aside in the refrigerator 20 minutes.
2. Meanwhile prepare the water smoker. No wood required this time, just fill up the water reservoir, and plug in the smoker. Lay out the duck legs on the racks, brush with more sauce and cook, covered, for 2– 2½ hours. Turn the legs over now and then and brush with the sauce, especially 30 minutes before they are done.
3. Remove the duck legs from the smoker, and serve hot with coleslaw and macaroni salad.

TAKE CARE WITH MARINADES

I've repeated this bit of information that appeared in the Big Game section so that marinades won't "repeat" on you—or worse. Besides adding flavor and moisture to meats, marinades are reuseable. You can use them 3–4 times, over the course of a week, for marinating other meats—as long as you keep it refrigerated.

Or you can double dip at one meal—using the marinade for a sauce at the table—as long as you take one precaution. Once your meat is on the grill, pour the marinade off into a saucepan and bring it to a boil; lower the heat, and cook at a low boil for 4 minutes. This ensures that any bacteria present in the raw meat (commercial as well as wild) will not make its way, alive, to your plate.

SLOW-SMOKED DUCK IN MAPLE GINGER GLAZE

Yield: 2 servings

I've become quite addicted to my water smoker since I bought it 6 months ago. Flavors range from the sharp bite of hickory and mesquite to the soothing tones of cherry and apple wood. And, being electric, it's virtually work free. (This glaze is symptomatic: I can't leave well enough alone. It's also delicious.)

Slow-Smoked Duck in Maple Ginger Glaze

Ingredients
3–4 chunks apple wood
¼ cup (60 ml) maple syrup
1 teaspoon crystallized ginger chunks
1 teaspoon orange zest
1 mallard, cleaned

Preparation
1. Two hours ahead, set the apple wood chunks in a pail of water.
2. In a small bowl, combine the maple syrup and crystallized ginger. Crush the ginger crystals into the syrup. Add the orange zest and set the glaze aside.

Cooking
1. Set up the water smoker. Drain the wood chunks and nestle them into the fake coals. (If you are using a charcoal-fired water smoker, heat the unit up to 240° F/115° C and add the chunks.) Fill the reservoir with water.
2. Dry the duck with paper towels, and brush some of the glaze over the bird. Set it in the smoker and close the lid. Cook for 2 hours, brush more glaze over the bird and cook another 30 minutes. Remove the bird from the smoker and serve hot with mashed potatoes (with 1–2 tablespoons of sour cream and Parmesan cheese added), or chill and slice up for appetizers.

SPICED DUCK

Yield: 2 servings

I like ducks; I like Madeira. And I love dried fruits. You aren't going to get away from my kitchen without having all three on one plate.

Spiced Duck

Ingredients

1 ½ pound (¾ kg) mallard, whole, cleaned

1 stick cinnamon (4 inches/10 cm)

⅔ cup (160 ml) Madeira

1 cup (250 ml) water

1 teaspoon chicken bouillon granules

½ cup (125 ml) chopped and packed mixed dried fruits

1 tablespoon honey

Cooking

1. Preheat a propane barbecue for 10 minutes, then turn down to medium. Or start 4 dozen charcoal briquettes, wait 25 minutes, and when you cannot keep your hand at the cooking level for more than 5–6 seconds, the fire is ready. An oven thermometer should register about 400° F (205° C) on the upper shelf.

2. Dry the mallard inside and out and place the cinnamon stick inside the body cavity. Set a shallow aluminum pan on the upper shelf of the barbecue and set the duck in it, breast side up. Close the lid and cook about 40–50 minutes, until a meat thermometer inserted into the thickest part registers 130° F (54° C) for rare, 140° F (60° C) for medium.

3. Meanwhile, in the house, combine the Madeira, water, bouillon granules, dried fruits, and honey in a medium-sized saucepan. Bring the mixture to a slow boil, then turn the heat down to a simmer. Cook about 15 minutes, until the liquid is sappy looking and is reduced by about one-half in volume.

4. When the duck is done, cut it into serving pieces, legs and breast, discard the cinnamon stick, and spoon some of the fruit compote over the grilled bird.

BEER-SMOKED SCAUP

Yield: 4 servings

If you like the distinct flavor of diving ducks, grill them up quick with a bit of salt and pepper. But if you have a problem with the livery flavor, try a beer smoke. It works on those strong saltwater ducks, too.

Beer-Smoked Scaup

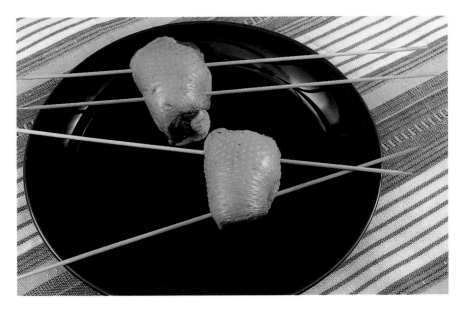

Ingredients
4 small diving ducks
24 ounces (700 ml) honey porter
2 cups (500 ml) water
2 teaspoons salt
1 teaspoon pepper

Preparation
1. Pluck the breasts of the ducks. Leaving the skin on, breast the birds out; a scaup breast—technically, both sides—weighs about 4 ounces (100 g), which is about right for one person. (Skin the legs out and save them for sausage. You can bone them later when you have a season's-worth of legs.) Dry with paper towels.
2. Pour the porter into a deep bowl or resealable plastic bag, then add the breasts. Marinate 24 hours in the refrigerator.

Cooking
1. Remove the breasts from the marinade, and save the marinade. In an electric water smoker, fill the water reservoir with the porter and an additional 2 cups (500 ml) of water, and plug it in to preheat. For a charcoal water smoker, follow the manufacturer's directions for achieving a cooking temperature of 220°–240° F (105°–115° C), then do as above.
2. While the smoker preheats, pat the duck breasts dry with paper towels. Carefully roll them up, overlapping the skin by an inch (2 ½ cm), and fasten with a wooden skewer. Stretch the skin a bit, so it covers most of the meat, and season with salt and pepper. Place the rolled breasts over the water reservoir, then close the lid. Cook 1–1 ½ hours, or until the reservoir is about dry. Serve as an appetizer, or with mashed sweet and red potatoes.

Note: The one disadvantage to water smoking whole birds is that without high heat, the skin won't crisp up. But the problem is easy to solve: make a simple glaze by liquefying 1–2 tablespoons of jelly (depending on the size of the bird) and rub it on the breast and legs. Turkey, goose, duck, or pheasant, the sugar in the glaze will make a crisp, shiny finish to any smoked bird.

A flock of lesser scaup, with a light sprinkling of canvasbacks. (Photograph © Bill Marchel)

CIDER GOOSE BREAST

Yield: 4 servings

The tart taste of apple cider makes this goose dish a bit different from most. Notice that the marinade takes 48 hours to work. The rest is easy.

Ingredients
1 ½ cups (375 ml) apple cider
¾ cup (185 ml) cider vinegar
½ medium onion, minced
3 tablespoons oil, canola or vegetable preferred
1 ½ tablespoons Worcestershire sauce
1 teaspoon ground cinnamon
1 teaspoon dried leaf thyme
Breast of 1 goose
1 tablespoon cornstarch

Preparation
Two days ahead: Combine the cider, cider vinegar, onion, oil, Worcestershire sauce, cinnamon, and thyme in a food processor and blend. Dry the breast with paper towel, and place in a resealable plastic bag with the marinade. Refrigerate 48 hours.

Cooking
1. Remove the breast from the marinade and drain, reserving the marinade. Dry the breast with paper towel and set aside while you prepare the sauce.

2. To prepare the sauce: Place the reserved marinade in a small saucepan, add the cornstarch and stir until it is dissolved—while the marinade is still cold. Bring to a boil over high heat. Boil hard about 2 minutes, then lower the heat to a slow boil and continue cooking, until the sauce thickens (about 5 minutes). Set aside and keep warm.

3. Start 4 dozen briquettes, or preheat a propane barbecue and turn down to high heat. When the charcoals are white hot and you can only hold your hand at cooking level for 4–5 seconds, place the goose breast on the grill.

4. Starting with the skin side up, barbecue hot 5 minutes to a side for bloody rare; 7 minutes to a side for rare. (The centers will be bloody rare and rare; the thinner edges will be closer to rare and medium rare.) Let the breast sit 5–10 minutes, then carve across the grain. Serve with German potato salad.

GOOSE BREAST WITH TANGERINE AND ROSEMARY GLAZE

Yield: 4 servings

This recipe is for the rest of us who can't wait 2 days for a marinade to work. The tangerine makes the glaze sweet, the rosemary adds a tart flavor, and cooking the goose breast this quickly, of course, makes it rich and moist at the table.

Ingredients

¼ cup (60 ml) sugar
½ cup (125 ml) white vinegar
1 cup (250 ml) fresh tangerine juice (3 tangerines)
1 teaspoon dried rosemary spines
½ teaspoon salt
¼ teaspoon pepper
Breast of 1 goose

Canada geese. (Photograph © William H. Mullins)

Preparation

In a small saucepan, combine the sugar and vinegar over medium heat and boil for 5 minutes. Add the juice and simmer until the liquid is reduced by half. Remove from the heat and stir in the rosemary.

Cooking

1. Preheat a propane barbecue for 10 minutes, then turn down to medium high heat. Or start 40 briquettes, wait 25 minutes, and when you cannot hold your hand at cooking level for more than 4–5 seconds the fire is ready.

2. Dry the goose breast and season with the salt and pepper, on both sides. Place the goose on a lightly oiled cooking rack, skin side down, and cook 5–7 minutes, or until the skin is nicely browned. Turn the goose and brush it with the tangerine glaze. Cook another 7–10 minutes, 15 minutes total, for rare to medium rare, 17–20 minutes total for medium to medium well. Serve with corn relish and baked beans.

SPRING-CLEANING GOOSE WITH SMOKED GARLIC BREAD

Yield: 4 servings

I love dinners that cook themselves, so last spring when we were busy sawing dead limbs off our much-neglected cherry and apple trees, I had a bright idea. The wood was already dead, and with a water smoker, we could be cooking dinner while we cleaned up the yard. (Better yet, start the goose before you go out on a partridge hunt.) Best part is that the timing is not so critical with a smoker as it is with direct cooking over a grill. Leave the goose 20 minutes longer than you expected and it won't suffer at all.

Spring-Cleaning Goose with Smoked Garlic Bread

Ingredients
3 chunks dry cherry wood
2 tablespoons cherry jelly
$\frac{1}{2}$ teaspoon cinnamon
1 goose, cleaned
1 head garlic, whole and unpeeled
2 tablespoons butter, softened
1 loaf Italian bread

Preparation
1. Soak the cherry wood in a bucket for 2 hours.
2. Liquefy the cherry jelly in a microwave or double boiler. Add the cinnamon, stir well, and set aside. This glaze will make the goose skin crisp and shiny.

Cooking
1. In an electric water smoker, place the drained wood chips on the fake coals, fill the reservoir with water, and place the goose on the upper shelf. Brush or rub the glaze across the top of the bird. When you are done tending the goose, set the head of garlic on the rack a few inches away from the goose. Cover the smoker. Cook about $2\frac{1}{2}$ hours, applying the glaze again 30 minutes before the bird is done. (If you are using a charcoal smoker, follow the manufacturer's directions to reach a smoking temperature of 240° F (115° C).
2. Remove the bird from the smoker and let it set 10 minutes before carving. While the bird sets, peel and trim the garlic and place it on a serving plate. Split the bread in half lengthwise, apply the butter lightly to each half, and set the bread, butter side down, on the hot grill. When the bread is thoroughly warmed, slice up the goose and serve it with smoked garlic spread on the Italian bread.

ROAST GOOSE WITH PHEASANT AND APPLE SAUSAGE STUFFING

Yield: 4–6 servings

This is about as traditional as a goose in a barbecue gets. Spike the stuffing with your own Pheasant and Apple Sausage (see recipe on page 115), use commercial chicken sausage, or just use your own favorite stuffing recipe. You'll need about 1 cup of dressing for each pound of oven-ready bird.

Ingredients
12 ounces (360 g) sausage, cubed
2 tablespoons butter or margarine
2¼ cups (560 ml) diced celery
1½ cups (375 ml) diced onion
2¼ cups (560 ml) dry bread cubes
1½ cups (375 ml) hot water
1½ teaspoons chicken bouillon granules
1 golden delicious apple, cored and sliced
   ¼ inch (½ cm) thick
5 pound (2½ kg) Canada goose, cleaned

Glaze
3 tablespoons butter or margarine, softened
1½ tablespoons brown sugar
¾ teaspoon curry powder

Preparation
1. Prepare the goose stuffing: In a large skillet brown the sausage in butter over medium high heat, then turn the heat down and add the celery and onion. Sauté the vegetables until they are soft. Stir in the bread cubes. In a small bowl, stir the bouillon granules into the hot water to dissolve, then add the bouillon to the skillet, gently moistening the stuffing mixture. Continue to sauté the stuffing until all of the excess moisture has been absorbed. Remove from the heat. Just before stuffing the bird, stir in the fresh apple slices.
2. Prepare the glaze: Combine the butter, brown sugar, and curry powder in a small bowl and stir to dissolve the dry ingredients. Set aside.

Cooking
1. Charcoal cooking, indirect method: Start 50 charcoal briquettes. Wait 25 minutes, then separate into two piles and place a drip pan (8x12 inches/20x30 cm) between them. Mound the coals on both long sides of the drip pan, evenly matching the heat. (The fire should be hot enough that you can only hold your hand 4–5 seconds at cooking level; 325° F/163° C for the overall temperature.) Replenish the coals (adding about 8 new coals to a side) as you start the goose to make sure the temperature stays constant throughout the cooking.

Propane, indirect method: Preheat one burner of the barbecue for 10 minutes, then turn the control down to medium low. This should give a constant 325°–350° F (163°–175° C) without having to replenish coals. Set a drip pan over the unlit burner.

2. When the coals are ready loosely stuff the goose with the sausage mixture. Tie the legs together with a length of cotton string, and snug them up against the body cavity to keep the stuffing inside. Tie the wings together, too, and wrap the string once around the breast so the wings stay close to the body and don't overcook. Wipe the glaze over the outside of the bird.

3. Place the bird on the cooking rack over the drip pan. Close the lid. Cook about 13–15 minutes per pound of bird; for a 5-pound goose, allow 65 minutes, and check with a meat thermometer. The stuffed goose is done when the thermometer reads 170° F (77° C). (The higher temperature is necessary because of the pork in the stuffing.)

4. To serve, remove the stuffing, then carve the goose. Serve with all the usual suspects: creamed onions, mashed potatoes, candied yams, pumpkin pie, and lots of fresh apple cider.

STUFFING SAFETY

Do not keep a stuffed bird waiting while the fire heats up, or store leftover stuffing inside the turkey or goose after it is cooked. The goose is just a vehicle for cooking the stuffing, not a fancy Tupperware container.

That's the safety warning; now here's what you really wanted to know. Allow about 1 cup of stuffing for each pound of ready-to-cook bird. Then stuff the bird loosely to allow all the stuffing to cook properly. Excess stuffing can be cooked in a buttered, covered, baking dish, during the last 45 minutes of cooking.

A blizzard of snow geese. (Photograph © Mark & Jennifer Miller Photos)

CHILLED PECAN-SMOKED GOOSE WITH RED PEPPER AIOLI

Specklebelly (or white-fronted) goose in Alberta wheat field.

Yield: 4–6 servings

Serve this smoked bird as an appetizer for New Year's Eve, or as a cool dinner some hot summer's eve. Either way, the smoked goose and aioli are a combination you won't forget.

Ingredients

1 cup (250 ml) pecan chips
5 pound (2½ kg) goose
⅔ cup (160 ml) mayonnaise
1 red bell pepper, cored and quartered
1 clove garlic
⅜ teaspoon red pepper flakes

Preparation

1. One day ahead: Cover the pecan chips with water and allow to soak 30 minutes. In an electric Little Chief smoker, smoke the goose 3 hours, using the moistened pecan chips a third at a time to smoke the goose. Then remove it from the smoker, wrap it well in foil, and place it in your oven at 350° F (175° C) to finish cooking; about 40 minutes. The goose is done when the meat thermometer inserted in the thickest part of the breast registers 140° F (60° C) for medium rare, 150° F (66° C) for medium. Chill overnight.
2. Several hours ahead: Combine the mayonnaise, red pepper, garlic, and red pepper flakes in a blender or food processor and purée. Chill.
3. To serve: Slice the goose thinly, and arrange on a platter around a bowl of the aioli dip.

SAUSAGE RECIPES

Anyone who has ever hunted with me knows how much I love prepared meats. From Polish sausage to liverwurst, fresh Italian sausage to hard salami, if I could eat only one food for the rest of my life, I'd be happy. But. Every time I eat prepared meats, my feet and hands puff up—especially when the thermometer rises above freezing. Mostly it's the salt, but the nitrates and nitrites, as well as the unsavory assortment of odd body parts used in commercial sausages, is simply not very appetizing. Then, too, it's hard, these days, to justify the 30–40 percent saturated fat in any food we eat. For years, I assumed that the fat and the salt were essential to the flavor I loved. I compromised by allowing myself to buy that stuff as long as I was hunting hard in cold weather. I figured I was working off the fat, and, in cold weather, the salt doesn't affect me as much. Besides, everyone knows that fat helps people keep warm in severe cold. That's why the Inuits eat blubber; why fresh caribou eyeball is a delicacy they rarely share with guests from warmer climes.

Bull elk. (Photograph © George Robbins Photo)

Then three years ago I was in Europe. Every morning there were fresh delicious European breads, fruit, and the tantalizing slab of meat on my plate; every walking tour passed a string of street venders with fresh, region du jour wursts. In a short 24 hours, I decided to throw caution to the wind and sample at least one local delight. I tried Prague ham, expecting the usual consequences: indigestion all night; feet and hands swollen in the morning. When I awoke, nothing. I ate Prague ham again, then a bit of wurst in Thuringia, and nothing again. I came back home and ate one brat. It took four double-strength antacids to get to sleep, and the next morning my feet were burning, swollen, and stuffed with water. I reveled in my misery, because at last I had found the truth: It wasn't the wurst; it was the cook.

I began collecting books, rare and far between, on

making homemade sausage. I bought a grinder, which turned out to have only one stuffer tub, which made it possible to use only large casings, and a motor that bogged down completely when I tried to grind a little saturated pork fat. I listened to anyone who would talk. In one particularly yuppie cooking store, I talked with one young woman whose father had worked in a sausage factory—and discovered apple pheasant sausage. And then I just dug in. Starting with the simplest fresh sausage patties, and growing into five smokers, a second refrigerator, and becoming a frequenter of butchering establishments, I learned how to make a bratwurst that depended on herbs and spices rather than salt for flavor, was lower in fat than the store stuff, and was a lot cheaper to produce. Now I eat these delicious prepared meats any time I want with impunity. And, I never run out of hot dog anymore while I still have a handful of bun.

Sausage Making Made Easy
Venison Trimming
You can use any cut of any animal for sausage. From forkhorn whitetail to rutty old elk, sweet tasting meat can be used for any recipe, while gamier tasting animals and cuts are best for spicier sausage. If you have a commercial processor grind the meat, ask them not to add suet to the venison. But it is best to do the grinding yourself because you will be much more ruthless about trimming. Cut away any bloodshot, dry, or discolored meat, as well as all venison fat. Venison fat is not like beef or pork fat; rather than being sweet, it has a tendency to taste like mutton tallow. Rely on the small amounts of pork in these recipes for the fat. The pork will make your sausage taste much better than the venison fat would have both when the sausage is fresh and after a 3–4 month sojourn in the freezer.

Page 99: *Whitetail buck. (Photograph © Mark & Jennifer Miller Photos)*

Cuts to Use: Where Do You Find Tough Meat for Sausage?

Deer, antelope, or elk, all venison animals, like beef, are most tender at the top of the rear quarters. Cut farther front, or farther down the animal, and the meat gets tougher. (Even the tenderloin is more tender toward the rear quarters than the front, although the loins are tender overall. It's usually not an issue.)

If you want a good balance of steaks, roasts, burger, sausage, and stew meat in the freezer, make your first roast the tenderloin, then take the top of each front and rear quarter for rolled shoulder and rump roasts, respectively; tender steaks are just below the roasts. Potential sausage should be taken from the area below these steaks and above the first leg joint. Any meaty scraps trimmed to make neater roasts and steaks, as well as the brisket on deer and the neck meat, may also be added to the grinder. Take a fillet knife to the bones and get as much meat as possible.

Just above the knee, where the muscles groups are long, skinny, and well used, the meat is tougher and full of sinew. Cut this into chunks for stew rather than saving it for the grinder. This is a matter of economics as well as taste: Most home grinders will not last long if you put this lower, sinewy meat through it on a regular basis; and most stews taste better cooked longer. Sinewy meat holds together better.

That's for young and tender animals. But what about the desperation-day deer you shot in the last legal light of hunting season, or the trophy buck whose antlers you fell in love with at first sight, but who may not have as much meat over the ribs as you'd hoped for in table fare? First of all how do you tell? Sometimes a skinny animal can taste and cut great—and a fatter animal can be under more stress.

There's only one secret to good game: Don't leave anything to guesswork. That first night after the kill, or when you get home, shower, and have a few minutes to sit down and rest your weary back, cut a small steak (4 ounce/100 g) off the front quarter. Not up on the shoulder blade—which you may want to be a rolled roast—and not below the knee. Take the steak from the thick section in between (see page 10 for details on the shoulder steak test). Then quick-fry it in a cast iron skillet on high heat with 2 tablespoons of butter. A 1-inch-thick (2½-cm-thick) steak will be rare to me-

Chukar. (Photograph © William H. Mullins)

dium rare when cooked 3–5 minutes to a side.

Cut into it with a standard table knife—not your hunting knife—and taste. Did it cut easily? Does it taste good? If you're two for two, do whatever you want with the animal: from party roasts to thuringer. If it's tough, let it age 5–7 days at 35°–55° F (1–13° C) in a clean, well-lighted place. If it's still tough after that, keep the rump roasts and rear-quarter round steaks, loin roasts, and back straps—as usual—but grind the shoulder and the rest of the nonstew meat for burger and sausage.

Birds

While you can use virtually any venison animal for the venison sausage recipes in this section, birds vary more in flavor. Milder tasting birds like turkey, mountain grouse, and chukar are better for the lightly spiced Wild Turkey and Sage Sausage (see recipe on page 115), while the Pheasant and Apple Sausage (see recipe on page 115) can be made with a combination of legs and breasts from pheasants, as well as any moderately dark-meated bird like Hungarian partridge, dove, and quail. Save the really strong tasting birds like sage and sharptail grouse for the lightly smoked sausages.

Start by breasting the birds, and pulling all the meat off the rest of the carcass; run the boned meat through the fine plate of your meat grinder and mix with the rest of the ingredients. Use fresh birds if you want—there's no need to age them if you're going to grind and spice them into sausage anyway. But for better taste, treat sausage-bound birds as you would any other bird. Draw the bird in the field, then rinse with clean cool water to remove as much of the blood as possible, and place on ice—within 2 hours on warm days—for the ride home. To get a good balance of bird and spice, it's important for the bird to cool properly and the meat to be free of contaminants. No matter what the species or recipe, blood and dirt always detract from the flavor of the meat.

In a pinch, substitute cottontail rabbit for the delicate white-meated birds, and jackrabbits for the stronger tasting ones. In dire straits, pad the recipe with grocery-store chicken. (If you need more than 3 pounds/ 1½ kg of filler, buy a small turkey. For that weight, it's more energy and cost efficient.)

We generally make bird sausage from last year's birds, as we get tuned up for this year's hunting. To tell the truth, I am much better at pointing a rifle than I am at the gentle art of swinging a shotgun. But even for bang-bang-damn shooters like me, there are always a few leftovers in the freezer, and waiting until the eve of the new season eliminates the feeling that I should save them for loftier meals. If you are an avid bird hunter and a sure shot, sausage adds welcome variety to a bountiful harvest.

Cottontail rabbit. (Photograph © Mark & Jennifer Miller Photos)

Pork

Since all of these recipes include a measure of pork, let's go over some basic ground rules. There's more than one reason ancient Judaic and Muslim societies banned pork for human consumption. With modern freezers and refrigerators, plenty of clean running water, and common sense, we can override some of pork's time-honored concerns. But there are still a few things to remember:

1. Once the pork is added to the sausage mix, you must treat the whole batch like pork.
2. Keep the mix cold: Starting with the meat slightly frozen—stiff, but not a solid block—not only prevents bacterial growth, but keeps the meat's own moisture from evaporating away. Thus a moister sausage. At every break, return the meat to the freezer. Do not let it sit out on the counter while you measure the spices or answer the phone. Do not make sausage on very hot days unless you live in an air-conditioned house.
3. Keep all utensils that touch the mix ultraclean: Between grindings, wash the grinder parts, bowls, spoons—everything that touches the ground meat—in hot, soapy water. Rinse the cutting board with boiling water, after washing it first in hot soapy water.
4. Never taste-test raw sausage: If you own a microwave, place a teaspoon of the mix on a plate, and cook on high for 1 minute at 500 watts (40 seconds at 700 watts) or until the sausage is well done. On a conventional range, fry a small amount of sausage over medium high heat until no pink remains.
5. To thaw any meat: Transfer from the freezer to the refrigerator 24–36 hours before using. Use a microwave on the defrost setting to speed the process, but never completely thaw any meat at room temperature.
6. To cook sausage made with pork: Always cook the sausage well done, or until no pink remains inside.

When adding pork to the sausage mix, you must think ahead. The rules for pork were the same for my mother and grandmother as they are for you and me. Trichinosis is no joke, but it can be avoided. For the cooked sausages in this section, follow the above pork strictures. Cooking the meat well will protect you. For the dry sausage, buy "certified" pork, that is, commercial pork certified to be trichinosis free, or else prefreeze the pork you will use.

To prefreeze: Cut the meat into 1-inch-thick (2½-cm-thick) strips, and lay them out in a single layer on a cookie sheet or baking pan. Cover, and freeze at -5° F (-20° C) for 20 days; -10° F (-23° C) for 10 days; or -20° F (-29° C) for 6 days. Check your freezer with a refrigerator-freezer thermometer. My chest freezer, on medium setting, runs at -5° F (-20° C); the freezer section of my refrigerator, on it's coldest setting, only gets down to 12° F (-11° C). It's not a bad idea to check your freezer every now and then anyway. For high quality and longevity, all meats should be stored at a minimum of 0 to -5° F (-18 to -20° C).

One more word about pork. I've used three kinds of pork in these recipes: side pork, bacon, and pork butt. Side pork is taken from the lower ribs—or side—of the pig and looks like pale bacon; bacon is side pork that has been salted and cured. Bacon is a bit of a cheater in sausage making; it adds a slightly smoky flavor without going to the trouble of smoking the sausage. Pork butt is a shoulder roast, cut front and high on the shoulder. It is economical and has a good fat-to-lean ratio for sausage making. When grinding the pork butt, cut it into strips to fit easily into the grinder funnel, and use both fat and meat. (Pork fat is very dense. If you are using a standard, home-use grinder, it may bog down. If it does, cut the fat into 1–2-inch/2½–5-cm cubes, then process.)

These recipes make a leaner sausage than you can buy in the store.

How do I know? I cooked an equal amount of store-bought bratwurst and homemade bratwurst, 5½ ounces (140 g), in identical cast iron skillets, over the same heat. Once cooked, they each lost about 1 ounce (25 g) in weight, but the store brat was lying in 1 tablespoon of rendered fat. The homemade brat, the Bear Brats recipe (see recipe on page 112), not only wasn't sitting in fat, but I had to reseason the cast iron pan. Despite that, everyone I've fed them to rates the Bear Brats A-1. So who needs to leave good money in the bottom of the skillet?

Types of Sausage
This cookbook includes three types of sausage: fresh, smoke-cooked, and dry. With fresh sausage, you grind the meat, mix in the spices, cook over a direct heat source, and eat it immediately. Smoke-cooked sausage is pretty much the same thing, but you cook over indirect heat, which takes longer, and you add water-soaked wood chips to the coals while cooking. Smoke-cooked sausage should be eaten within 2–3 days after cooking. The Venison Salami (see recipe on page 123) is a dry sausage and is a bit more work. This one is slow smoked for 12 hours in an aluminum Little Chief smoker, which is about the only way you can predictably control the temperature over that long of a cooking process. But dry sausage will last longer in the refrigerator: 1–2 weeks.

To Stuff or Not to Stuff
Except for the slow-smoked sausage, you can cook many of these sausages as patties or cased, whichever you prefer. Patties can be harder to handle on the grill, but with either a length of aluminum foil—perforated a few times—or a hinged burger grate, that problem can be solved.

Patty makers have several options:

1. Freeze the sausage like burger, in 1–2 pound packages, depending on the size of your family. Then thaw and shape into patties before cooking.
2. Shape the sausage into patties, and stack with waxed paper between each portion. Wrap the stack in aluminum foil and freeze.
3. Shape a pound of sausage at a time into logs, like commercial breakfast sausage, and freeze. (The easiest way to do this is to place a length of plastic wrap on the counter, center the sausage loosely, then shape, rolling the mixture inside the wrap.) To use, thaw partially,

Patties or links? Sometimes it doesn't matter. Here are Wild Turkey and Sage Sausage in patties, with Pheasant and Apple Sausage in link form.

then slice into individual servings and cook on the grill in a hinged grate, on perforated aluminum foil, or directly on the grill. (Be sure to oil the cool grill before cooking any meat, to prevent sticking.)

You have several options in casings, as well:

1. Natural casings: these come most commonly in hog, but are also available in synthetic lamb. Hog casing usually comes packed in salt and is frozen in a resealable bag. (Synthetic lamb casing is dry.) One bag makes about 50 pounds (25 kg) of sausage: 1 foot (30 cm) of hog casings to 1 pound ($\frac{1}{2}$ kg) of meat; 2 feet (61 cm) per pound ($\frac{1}{2}$ kg) for lamb casings. Hog casings produce the traditional bratwurst look—a sausage about $1\frac{1}{2}$ inches ($3\frac{3}{4}$ cm) in diameter; lamb is the traditional breakfast link sausage thickness, about 1 inch ($2\frac{1}{2}$ cm) in diameter. Hog casings are readily available at meat counters in hunter-friendly country and fit those grinders that have only one stuffing tube. If you own a stuffer with two tubes, one of them is $\frac{5}{8}$ inch ($1\frac{1}{2}$ cm) for hog casings, and one is $\frac{3}{8}$ inch (1 cm) for lamb casings. If you want to have two different size sausages and don't own a stuffer with two tubes, check out your local sausage shop or a sausage maker's catalog.

To use natural casings, soak a length of the salted casings more than adequate to stuff the batch you have ready. (They're cheap; once you're set up to stuff, it is very annoying and time consuming to start over with the soaking process.) Soak the casings in clean, cold water for 90 minutes, then run fresh cold water through them just before stuffing. This makes them easier to stuff and eliminates most of the packing salt.

2. Synthetic casings: The synthetic variety require neither refrigeration nor salt and should be kept dry before using. They are, however, fragile and harder to find.

To use synthetic casings, simply place them over the stuffing tube and stuff.

The Tools

If you want a low-key sausage making experience, hog casings are easy to find, are easy to use, and can be stuffed with just about any type of sausage mix. For up to about 30 pounds ($13\frac{1}{2}$ kg) of sausage a year, the household meat grinders commonly available in catalogs and stores (which cost about $100 in 2000) will work. Some of those grinders come with one, some with two sizes of sausage stuffing tubes. If you want to stuff a variety of casings, be sure you have a tube with an inside diameter of $\frac{3}{8}$ inch (1 cm) for lamb, $\frac{5}{8}$ inch ($1\frac{1}{2}$ cm) for hog.

If, however, you want to develop a minor obsession, invest in a hard-core, heavy-duty grinder. It will cost three to five times as much but will be much more economical in the long run. Then get on the mailing list of some sausage maker's catalogs so you can order every variety of casing, spice, and recipe ever invented. Unless you get into one of these pipelines, advanced sausage making can get frustrating. It is a lot easier to buy a whole truckload of books on how to decorate your house for Christmas than just one that will teach you how to make delicious home sausage.

COARSE OR FINE: WHICH GRINDING PLATE IS BEST?

Here's where tradition runs face first into personal preferences. Just because the meat used for Polish sausage was always cut coarse, that doesn't mean it still has to be cut coarse. I may be the last person in the world you'd find sticking blindly to tradition, but over the years, I've found that I prefer Polish sausage ground coarse. I also prefer the traditional fine grind for hot dogs. (By the way, if you really want to go totally traditional, leave the grinder in the closet and cut your meats with a knife.)

Through this section, I've suggested either coarse or fine grind with sausages I feel really need one or the other, and I've left it up to you where it doesn't seem to make much difference at all. But, since you're making the sausage, you get to choose what you like best for all of them. The grind is controlled by the "plate," which has either large (for coarse grind) or small (for fine grind) holes, and which fits onto the front end of the grinder.

Tips for Beginners

1. To avoid bubbles at the beginning of the sausage string: Fit the casing over the spout with a 2–3 inch (5–7½ cm) overhang. Do not tie that end off yet. Press the meat through the grinder and let it fill the overhang. Then stop the machine, pinch off the sausage in the casing and squeeze that 2–3 inches out the open end of the casing. Return the sausage to the grinder, and tie off the casing. No bubble.

2. Let the casings come off the stuffing tube at an even pace, either on their own or by placing your thumb and index finger at the bottom and top of the stuffing tube. If the casings come off faster than they are filling, apply a little pressure to slow them down or you will end up with bubbles in the sausage. The bubbles will pop when cooking and spatter you with hot juices. But, restrict the casings, either by holding them too tight, or by having the casings stick on the stuffer tube, and the sausage will tear and you'll have to cut that casing off and start over.

If you get bubbles in your sausage, just pierce them with a fork before cooking as well as before freezing them. In the freezer, the bubbles—and the air they're made of—will case premature freezer burn.

3. When twisting the filled casings to lengths: Twist the same direction for each length of sausage, as it comes out of the tube. This way you won't untwist the last length in doing the next.

4. For more uniform lengths of hot dogs, brats, etc.: Stuff the entire length of the casing without twisting. Then, when you're done with that batch, or that individual length of casing, lay the sausage out on the kitchen counter alongside a ruler. Measure and twist at whatever lengths you desire.

5. To get as much of the sausage mix into the casings as possible: At the end of the batch, when it's all in the grinder but there's not enough sausage left to push it out, run 2 slices of bread through the grinder as the caboose. Watch the end of the stuffing tube: When the mix turns white, that's the bread; squeeze off the sausage. For pale-meated bird sausage, use 2 slices of dark bread, so you'll clearly see when the meat turns to bread. The bread will also scour the inside of the grinder and make cleanup a lot easier.

EXTENDING THE FREEZER LIFE OF SAUSAGE

A sausage has two strikes against it no matter how well you wrap it for the freezer. First, sausage is full of fat, and fat, no matter what variety, simply doesn't survive long in the freezer. Second, sausage is made of ground meat. And ground meat, because it has so much more exposed surface area than a large roast, for instance, also has a larger amount of surface area that can be reached—and affected—by cold air.

To combat these disadvantages you can do several things. Begin by tightly double-wrapping the sausage packages in good freezer paper, being careful to squeeze out all the air, in as large a quantity as is practicable for your family. If you're trying to keep the sausage past 4 months, you should first use a layer of plastic wrap, then the freezer paper. If possible, store the sausage in a chest freezer, and keep the thermostat at 0 to -5° F (-18 to -20° C). Why a chest freezer? It keeps the cold environment constant. Trust me; I've tested all three types of freezers.

The freezer above your refrigerator operates at 10° F (-12° C), which isn't cold enough for prolonged storage. And, though an upright freezer can reach the correct temp, both refrigerator-freezers and uprights are built on the vertical: Open the door and the cold falls out. Literally. Once the cold falls out, the warm room air rushes in to take its place. A chest freezer, on the other hand, can be open more than 4 minutes before it starts to lose cold.

To lengthen the freezer life of your sausages (up to 6 months) without losing quality:

1. Remove all air when wrapping.

2. Double (or triple) wrap all packages.

3. Reduce the amount of exposed surface area as much as possible by wrapping in large quantities.

4. Use a chest freezer at 0° to -5° F (-18 to -20° C). If you don't have a chest freezer, severely limit the frequency and length of time you leave the freezer door open.

TO STUFF SAUSAGE INTO HOG CASING

1. Soak casings in clean cold water until soft, about 90 minutes. If you are using synthetic lamb casing, skip to Step 3.

2. Pretend you're filling a water balloon: Attach one end of a length of casing to the water faucet. Then run cold water through the casing. These first two steps eliminate most of the salt used to preserve the casing.

3. Wipe the end of the sausage stuffing tube with a small amount of vegetable oil. Starting with one end of the casing, load as much of the casing as you can onto the stuffing tube.

4. Grab hold of the loose end of the casing, and start the grinder. When the sausage starts coming out the end, stop the motor, pinch off about the first 2 inches of sausage, and toss it back into the grinder. Then tie off the front end of the casing.

5. Now fill the rest of the casing, squeezing it off again to leave a 2–3-inch (5–7½-cm) tag to tie off that end of the sausage.

6. Turn the sausage as you fill the casing and it will not bind.

7. To make this one long string of sausage into individual servings, twist the casings at evenly spaced intervals: 4–6 inches (10–15 cm) for brats, 8 inches (20 cm) for hot dogs. Or choose whatever length you want your sausages to be so that they fill—or overfill—your rolls.

6. Do your casings break on stuffing? Loosen up on the casing as it comes off the tube. You are overstuffing.

7. Do you have air pockets? Keep a tighter rein on the casings feeding off the tube. You are understuffing.

8. Does the sausage break apart while on the grill? Poke a hole in the casing before cooking. Breaking apart can be a sign of overstuffing, or a sign you need to handle the sausage more gently.

9. What do you do with that last smidgen of sausage when you're out of casing? Break it up into your hash browns, or brown it in the frying pan before adding your scrambled eggs next morning; add it to your next soup or stew; or better yet, add an equal amount of cooked rice, stuff the mixture into a sweet bell pepper, and roast it on the grill for a well-deserved snack.

Start with the fresh sausages—Traditional Breakfast, Whitetail Italian, Mule Deer Polish Sausage, hot dogs, and brats. Then go on to the smoked. In our grandparent's days, everyone made sausage. It's not terribly hard, and it can be very satisfying. But most of all, it should be delicious.

Once you own a grinder, the rest of the sausage makings are cheap and easy to acquire. Ask at your local butcher shop.

TO FIND SAUSAGE-MAKING INGREDIENTS AND EQUIPMENT

Casings and sausage-making ingredients can be bought at your local grocery (hog casings in salt are most common), and at butcher shops. Equipment can be found in kitchen stores and through sausage-making catalogs (listed to the right). I have tried to keep these recipes limited to readily available ingredients, processed with readily available tools. If, however, you can't find something, or if you get really wild and need obscure or hard-to-find spices, try the mail-order places listed to the right.

Mail Order Spice House LTD
POB 1633
Milwaukee, WI 53201
414-272-0977

Penzeys Spices
POB 933
Muskego, WI 53150
414-679-7207

The Sausage Maker, Inc.
1500 Clinton Street, BLDG. 123
Buffalo, NY 14206
716-824-5814

FRESH SAUSAGES

TRADITIONAL BREAKFAST SAUSAGE

Yield: $1\frac{1}{4}$ pounds ($\frac{3}{5}$ kg)

Whether you take the barbecue along on camping trips or cook over an open fire, make this sausage. The fire will add a rich, crisp touch to an old favorite.

Mule deer buck surveying his domain. (Photograph © Michael H. Francis)

Ingredients
1 pound ($\frac{1}{2}$ kg) venison
$\frac{1}{4}$ pound ($\frac{1}{8}$ kg) side pork
1 teaspoon ground sage
1 teaspoon dried leaf thyme
1 tablespoon dried parsley flakes
$\frac{1}{2}$ teaspoon salt
$\frac{3}{4}$ teaspoon pepper

Preparation
1. Run the venison and side pork, separately, through the fine plate of a grinder. Combine, and run through grinder together. Place in a large bowl.
2. Add the sage, thyme, parsley, salt, and pepper. Mix thoroughly by hand, and run one more time through the grinder for a fine-textured breakfast sausage. Stuff into lamb-sized casings or shape into patties.

Cooking
1. Start 40 briquettes, or preheat a propane barbecue for 10 minutes and turn down to medium high. For charcoal, begin to cook when the charcoals are white hot and you can only hold your hand at cooking level for 4–5 seconds. Lightly oil the sausages and place them (cased or patties) on the grill.
2. For sausages that are 1 inch ($2\frac{1}{2}$ cm) thick, cook 15 minutes, turning often, until the outsides are browned and the insides no longer pink. Serve with pancakes and eggs.

WHITETAIL ITALIAN SAUSAGE

Yield: $2\frac{1}{4}$ pounds ($1\frac{1}{8}$ kg)

A plateful of Italian sausage wrapped around a heaping mound of spaghetti is one of my favorite winter meals. Make the sausage, and make plenty, for this and the deliciously different barbecued pizza that follows.

Ingredients

1 tablespoon plus $\frac{1}{2}$ teaspoon fennel seed
$1\frac{1}{4}$ teaspoons black peppercorns
$\frac{3}{4}$ cup (185 ml) Chianti
2 teaspoons dried leaf oregano
3 cloves garlic
$\frac{1}{2}$ teaspoon sugar
$\frac{2}{3}$ teaspoon non-iodized salt
1 pound ($\frac{1}{2}$ kg) venison
$1\frac{1}{4}$ pound ($\frac{3}{5}$ kg) pork butt

Preparation

1. Combine the fennel seeds and peppercorns in a blender with the Chianti, oregano, garlic, sugar, and salt. Purée until the fennel seeds and peppercorns are coarsely chopped.
2. Run the venison and pork separately, once, through the fine plate of a grinder. Combine the ground meat with the puréed seasoning mix in a large bowl and mix thoroughly by hand. Grind one more time through the fine plate. Stuff into hog-sized casings, or make into patties.

Cooking

Start 40 briquettes, or preheat a propane barbecue and turn down to medium high. When the charcoals are white hot and you can only hold your hand at cooking level for 4–5 seconds, lightly rub each sausage with oil and place them (cased or patties) on the grill. For sausages that are $1\frac{1}{2}$ inches ($3\frac{3}{4}$ cm) thick, cook 15 minutes, until the outsides are browned and the insides no longer pink. Pile your serving platter high with spaghetti and meatless tomato sauce, then wrap the Italian sausage around it. Serve with garlic bread and fresh green salad.

Barbecued Pizza

Yield: 12-inch (30-cm) pizza—serves 4

Now that you have all that Italian sausage, what are you going to do with it? Well, here's an idea: pizza. Use a ready-to-use pizza bread round, and, for convenience, 2 hinged grates (9x9 inches/22x22 cm each). The elephant garlic used in this recipe is a much milder version of the old favorite and is perfect for the grill because of its larger size. It won't fall through the grate as easily.

Barbecued Pizza

Ingredients

3 cloves elephant garlic, sliced ¼ inch
  (½ cm) thick
5 Roma or plum tomatoes, halved
1 medium yellow onion, sliced ¼ inch
  (½ cm) thick
1 green bell pepper, cut in ¼-inch (½-cm)
  strips
4 large mushrooms, about ¼ pound (⅛ kg),
  sliced ¼ inch (½ cm) thick
½ pound (¼ kg) Italian sausage, cut ½ inch
  (1 cm) thick
3 tablespoons olive or canola oil
2 teaspoons dried leaf oregano
1 prepared pizza bread shell (1 pound/½ kg)
4 ounces (100 g) mozzarella cheese, grated
¼ cup (60 ml) grated Parmesan cheese

Preparation

1. Preheat a propane barbecue for 10 minutes, then turn down to medium high heat. Or start 40 briquettes, wait 25 minutes, and start cooking when you can't hold your hand above the heat for more than 4–5 seconds.

2. While the barbecue heats up, place the vegetables and sausage slices in the hinged grates, setting the garlic slices on the tomato halves to keep them moist. In a small bowl, combine the oil and oregano and lightly brush the vegetables and sausage before you begin cooking.

Cooking

Place the grates on the grill, and cook about 20 minutes, turning often. Gently place the pizza shell on a rack away from the direct fire, preferably above the hinged grates, for the last 8 minutes of cooking. Remove both the grates and the pizza shell from the grill, arrange the vegetables and sausage on the pizza crust, and top with first the mozzarella, then the Parmesan cheese.

Recipe note: If you don't have hinged grates, you can use skewers for the sausage and a length of heavy-duty aluminum foil—perforated liberally—to grill the vegetables.

Setting up the hinged grate for Barbecued Pizza.

MULE DEER POLISH SAUSAGE

Yield: 2 pounds

In truth, if you go to Poland, every region—probably every street corner—has its own sausage, and no one ever heard of "Polish" sausage. (Like no Frenchman ever heard of French toast and no Canadian, Canadian bacon.) So, I guess this is classic American Polish sausage, made with the classic American mule deer. A delicious way to treat my favorite denizen of the West.

Ingredients
1 pound (½ kg) venison
1 pound (½ kg) pork butt
4 cloves garlic, minced
2 teaspoons dried marjoram leaves
2½ teaspoons salt
¼ teaspoon cayenne pepper
1 teaspoon ground black pepper
1 quart (1 liter) pilsner beer
10 black peppercorns, whole

Preparation
1. Grind the meats with the coarse plate. In a large bowl, combine the ground meats with the garlic, marjoram, salt, cayenne, and ground black pepper. Mix thoroughly by hand and stuff in hog-sized casing.
2. Cook immediately, or wrap tightly in freezer paper, and store in the freezer 3–4 months.

Cooking
1. Pierce the sausages in several places with a fork or sharp knife. Combine the beer, peppercorns, and several sausages in a medium-sized saucepan (with enough beer to allow the sausages to float freely). Bring to a boil. Reduce the heat to low, cover, and simmer about 20 minutes. Carefully remove the sausages from the beer and pat dry with paper towels.
2. Preheat your propane barbecue for 10 minutes, then lower the heat to medium high. Or start 40 briquettes and wait 25 minutes, until you cannot keep your hand at the cooking surface for more than 4–5 seconds. When the grill is ready, rub the sausages lightly with oil and place on the grill directly over the heat. Cook about 7–10 minutes, until the sausages are rich brown and heated through, turning often. Serve on kaiser rolls with stone-ground mustard.

BEAR BRATS

Yield: 1 pound (½ kg)

Bratwurst is a highly spiced, German sausage that complements bear's natural pork flavor. Use the bear's own fat if the animal was well padded and the meat tastes good; if not, use commercial pork for the fat. If you have no bear, use any venison. Even moderately gamy cuts will work well in this recipe.

Bear Brats

Ingredients
1 slice bread, cubed
⅓ cup (80 ml) milk
½ pound (¼ kg) bear meat
½ pound (¼ kg) pork butt (or 2 ounces/50 g bear fat with an equal amount more of bear meat)
1¼ teaspoon salt
1¼ teaspoon white pepper
1 teaspoon ground allspice
½ teaspoon ground sage
¼ teaspoon ground ginger

Preparation
1. Place the bread cubes in a shallow bowl, pour the milk over, and let sit for 5 minutes. In the meantime, grind the meat once through a fine plate. Place the ground meat in a large bowl.
2. Add the salt, pepper, allspice, sage, and ginger to the ground meat, then add the bread and mix thoroughly with your hands. Stuff in hog-sized casings.

Cooking
Start 40 briquettes, or preheat a propane barbecue and turn down to medium high to cook. When the coals are white hot, and you can hold your hand at cooking level for only 4–5 seconds, place the brats on the grill. Cook 15 minutes, until the outsides are browned and the insides are no longer pink. Serve on kaiser rolls with sweet hot mustard and sauerkraut.

Black bear. (Photograph © Michael H. Francis)

HOMEMADE VENISON HOT DOGS

Yield: 2 pounds (1 kg)

The first thing you'll notice about these dogs is that they aren't bright red, nor are they made of animal by-products. That's good. What's better is that you don't give up any of the traditional hot dog flavor just because you took the time to make them home-cooked healthy.

Ingredients

¾ cup (185 ml) finely chopped onion
3 cloves garlic
2 teaspoons ground coriander
1 teaspoon dried leaf marjoram
½ teaspoon ground mace
¾ teaspoon dry mustard
2 teaspoons sweet Hungarian paprika
2 tablespoons sugar
¼ cup (60 ml) cold water
1 pound (½ kg) venison
1 pound (½ kg) pork butt

Preparation

1. Combine the onion, garlic, coriander, marjoram, mace, mustard, paprika, sugar, and water in a blender or food processor and purée.
2. Grind the venison and pork meats through the fine plate of a grinder, once separately. Then combine the puréed seasoning mixture and ground meat thoroughly by hand and run through the grinder one more time. Stuff in lamb- or hog-sized casings, depending on what size you want your dogs. (Lamb casings will be the size of link sausage; hog, about the size of knockwursts.)

Cooking

Start 4 dozen briquettes or preheat a propane barbecue. When the charcoals are white hot and you can only hold your hand at cooking level for 4–5 seconds, lightly wipe the dogs with a bit of oil, then place them on the grill. Cook 15 minutes for hog casings (about 1½-inch/3¾-cm diameter), 10–12 for lamb casings (about ¾ inch/2 cm diameter), until the outsides are browned and the insides are no longer pink. Serve with mustard, relish, and raw onions on hot dog rolls.

Homemade
Venison Hot Dogs

WILD TURKEY AND SAGE SAUSAGE

Yield: 1 ¾ pounds (⁴⁄₅ kg)

This turkey sausage is easy enough for breakfast on your next hunting or camping trip, but tasty enough to barbecue the next time you have a late Sunday breakfast.

Ingredients
1 ½ pound (¾ kg) boned turkey meat
¼ pound (⅛ kg) side pork
1 teaspoon ground sage
½ teaspoon dried rosemary
1 teaspoon salt
½ teaspoon pepper

Preparation
1. Grind the boned turkey with the side pork into a large bowl. Add the sage, rosemary, salt, and pepper. Mix thoroughly by hand.
2. Shape into a long tube, about 2 inches (5 cm) in diameter, wrap in plastic wrap, and freeze. (To freeze longer than 24 hours, double wrap in freezer paper as well as the plastic wrap.)

Cooking
Partially thaw the sausage roll in the refrigerator. When the sausage will slice but is still firm, slice the roll into patties that are 1 inch (2 ½ cm) thick. Grill over a hot fire until the outside is a rich brown and the inside is no longer pink. Serve with a side of scrambled eggs and corn bread.

PHEASANT AND APPLE SAUSAGE

Yield: 1 ½ pound (¾ kg)

If you were fortunate enough to get lots of pheasants during hunting season, sacrifice one or two to make this sausage. Or keep the legs of all your paler, mild tasting birds separate in the freezer and make a leg sausage some cold winter night.

Ingredients
1 ¼ pound (³⁄₅ kg) pheasant meat
¼ pound (⅛ kg) bacon strips, partially frozen
2 red delicious apples, cored, seeded, and coarsely grated (about 1 ¼ cup/310 ml)
⅔ cup (160 ml) diced onion
3 teaspoons curry powder

Preparation
Grind the pheasant meat and bacon strips together into a large bowl. Add the apple, onion, and curry powder. Mix thoroughly by hand and stuff into hog-sized casings, or shape into patties.

Cooking
1. You can add this delicious wild bird sausage to your traditional Thanksgiving Day turkey stuffing or make a simple summer meal. Start 40 briquettes, or preheat a propane barbecue and turn down to medium high. When the charcoals are white hot and you can't hold your hand at cooking level for more than 4–5 seconds, or the propane unit is ready, lightly oil the sausages and place them on the grill.
2. Cook hog-cased sausages and patties about 15 minutes, until the outside is browned and the inside no longer pink. Serve with potato salad.

LIGHTLY SMOKED SAUSAGES

MEXICAN MULEY CHORIZO

Yield: 2 pounds (1 kg)

Cased chorizo is fine barbecued whole, or slice it for the skewer for your next venison kabob dinner.

Ingredients
1 pound ($\frac{1}{2}$ kg) mule deer meat
1 pound ($\frac{1}{2}$ kg) pork butt
3 teaspoons chili powder
3 teaspoons ground cumin
3 cloves garlic, minced
1 teaspoon crushed red pepper flakes
$\frac{1}{2}$ teaspoon cinnamon
$\frac{3}{4}$ teaspoon salt
$\frac{3}{4}$ teaspoon black pepper
3 tablespoons red wine vinegar
$\frac{3}{4}$ cup (185 ml) mesquite chips

Preparation
Run the mule deer and pork though the coarse plate of a grinder, once separately. Combine the ground meat with the chili powder, cumin, garlic, red pepper, cinnamon, salt, black pepper, and wine vinegar in a large bowl and mix thoroughly by hand. (Use rubber gloves to handle this hot mix.) Stuff into lamb-sized casings or make into patties.

Cooking
1. Soak the mesquite chips in cold water for 15–30 minutes. Meanwhile, start 40 charcoal briquettes, or preheat a propane barbecue and turn down to medium high. When the coals are white hot and you can only hold your hand at cooking level for 4–5 seconds, or when the propane unit is ready, drain the wood chips and strew over the hot coals. Wipe or brush the cased chorizo with a bit of oil (for patties, oil the rack before preheating the grill), place on the grill, and close the cover.
2. Cook 10 minutes for lamb casings (about $\frac{3}{4}$ inch/2 cm diameter) until the outsides are browned and insides no longer pink. Serve with salsa and chips as an appetizer, or with chili for dinner.

A big-necked, rutty old mule deer buck, just asking for Mexican Muley Chorizo. (Photograph © Mark & Jennifer Miller Photos)

WHITE SAUSAGE

Yield: 2 pounds (1 kg)

Like the Beatles's famous *White Album,* this sausage is bound to become a favorite. Make it with all white meats: pheasant breasts, chukar, mountain grouse—if you have enough—and cottontails. This year cottontails and pheasants are plentiful, so there will be lots of white sausage at our house.

Ingredients

1 ¼ pounds (³/₅ kg) white meat
½ pound (¼ kg) pork butt
2 slices dry white toast
½ cup (125 ml) cream
1 medium white onion, finely diced
2 teaspoons salt
1 teaspoon white pepper
2 eggs
½ teaspoon dried summer savory leaves
¼ teaspoon dried thyme leaves
¼ teaspoon dried basil leaves
¼ teaspoon dried tarragon leaves
¼ teaspoon dried rosemary, crushed
3 sprigs fresh oregano (each about 5 inches/ 12½ cm long)

Preparation

1. Grind the meats using a fine plate on the grinder. Set the meat aside in the refrigerator while you prepare the seasonings. In a small bowl, crumble the toast into the cream and set it aside to soak. In a large bowl combine the onion, salt, pepper, eggs, savory, thyme, basil, tarragon, and rosemary. Add the toast and cream mixture, and stir well into the seasonings.
2. Add the ground meat to the seasonings, mix thoroughly by hand, then stuff into hog-sized casings.

Cooking

1. Start 40 briquettes, or preheat a propane barbecue. When the briquettes are white hot, or the propane unit has preheated and been turned down to medium high, wipe the sausages with a little oil. Adjust the cooking rack to 2½–3 inches (6¼–7½ cm) above the heat. Lay the oregano sprigs on the coals just under the sausages as you lay them on the rack.
2. Cover the grill, and open the bottom and top vents partway to keep the fire hot. The cooking surface should be 425° F (220° C). Cook the sausages 15–20 minutes, turning occasionally to brown all sides. (A charcoal fire will take closer to 20 minutes, a propane one closer to 15, even with the cooking surface of both being the same.) Serve hot with potato salad and grilled corn on the cob.

CHEAP AND EASY BREAD CRUMBS

The easiest way to get 2 slices of dry toast is to begin the sausage recipe by sticking 2 slices of bread in the toaster. Then when the toast pops up, nicely browned, but not burned, ignore it. The toaster is the perfect place to dry out a slice or two of bread, as you've probably already learned by accident. Now you're doing it on purpose.

PEKING DUCK SAUSAGE

Yield: 1 ¾ pounds (⁴/₅ kg)

I guess it was inevitable that someday I would try to combine my favorite kind of hunting with my favorite type of food. If you don't like strong flavors, make this with dabbling ducks; if you love the more pungent flavors of divers, have at it. Or if you have an embarrassment of geese, a Canada could certainly make this Peking sausage. Whatever you do, don't add salt; between the bacon and the soy sauce, this is a tangy, flavorful sausage already.

Ingredients

1 pound (½ kg) boned duck meat
¼ pound (⅛ kg) bacon, half frozen
½ pound (¼ kg) side pork, half frozen
⅛ cup (30 ml) soy sauce
Juice of 1 medium-sized orange
1 teaspoon ground ginger
½ teaspoon pepper

Drake blue-winged teal. (Photograph © Jeffrey Rich Nature Photography)

Preparation

1. Grind the duck meat and bacon, once separately and once together, through the fine plate of your grinder. Set aside in the refrigerator while you prepare the seasonings.

2. In a large mixing bowl, combine the soy sauce, orange juice, ginger, and pepper, stirring until the ginger has dissolved. Pour the seasonings over the ground meats and mix thoroughly by hand. Stuff in hog-sized casings. This mixture is so moist it will be a little harder to stuff than other sausages, but the added moisture tastes great once it is cooked.

Cooking

1. In an electric water smoker: Soak 3 chunks of fruitwood (orange if you can get it) in water for 2 hours. Then drain the chunks and place them on the fake coals, being careful not to let them touch the element. Fill the reservoir with water.

2. Wipe the sausages with a light coating of oil, then place on the cooking rack. Cook at 220°–240° F (105°–115° C) about 2½ hours. Check with a meat thermometer. With the pork added, these sausages should be a minimum of 160° F (71° C) to eat safely. Serve hot, or chill and slice for appetizers.

3. You can also use a charcoal kettle grill or charcoal water smoker to cook the sausage. For the charcoal kettle grill, start about 4 dozen briquettes on one side of the grill. Then place a water pan on the other side and the sausage over the pan. Place the drained wood chunks on the coals when you start the sausage.

4. Maintain a constant temperature of 220°–240° C (105°–115° C) by opening or closing the vents as needed and adding one third more coals after each 30 minutes of cooking to keep the fire going. For the charcoal water smoker, follow the manufacturer's directions for achieving the constant hot-smoking temperature noted above.

WET-SMOKED SAUSAGES

SWEDISH KORV

Yield: 4½ pounds (2¼ kg)

A lot of recipes for korv include potato instead of barley, but this recipe comes from Mary and Ole Olson, who have been making korv with barley for years, and Ole is well known for never being wrong. He's also one of my favorite duck-blind partners, and I want to keep it that way.

Ingredients

2 pounds (1 kg) venison
1 pound (½ kg) pork butt
1 large onion, finely chopped
⅔ cup (160 ml) cooked barley
1 tablespoon salt
1 teaspoon pepper
⅛ cup (30 ml) water

Preparation

Grind the venison and pork together and combine with the onion, barley, salt, pepper, and water. Add more water, ⅛ cup (30 ml) at a time, if needed to make more moist. Stuff into hog-sized casings. Traditionally, korv is cased, then the ends are tied together with a square knot to make a ring. Rings can be any size to fit your individual needs and cooker.

Cooking

1. In an electric water smoker: Wipe a small amount of oil on the korv to prevent it from sticking to the grill. Fill the water pan, and place the korv on the grill. Cover and plug the cooker in.
2. Cook about 90 minutes, then test the korv by sticking a meat thermometer into but not through the sausage. Since the korv contains pork, it should be cooked to 160° F (71° C). Serve hot with mustard and boiled potatoes, or refrigerate and use as lunch meat and snacks.

THE BEST WAY TO COOK BARLEY

Yield: 3¾ cups (935 ml), cooked

Do not follow the directions on the bag of barley or you will end up with a water-sodden pile of paste. Instead, add 1½ cups (375 ml) of raw barley to 3 cups (750 ml) boiling water. When the water returns to a boil, lower the heat to a slow simmer, stir once with a fork to mix, and cover the pot. Cook 25 minutes until the grain is no longer crunchy but is still firm, and all of the water has been absorbed. Stir with a fork to keep the grains from sticking as they cool. Then set the barley in the refrigerator while you grind the meats. The barley should be room temperature or below before adding to the korv mixture.

TIMING WATER SMOKERS

Cooking time varies among water cookers and according to ambient air temperature. A charcoal smoker can be adjusted by adding or subtracting coals and by opening or closing the vents. Electric is less obliging, though more convenient. At 70° F (21° C) outside temperature, my electric water smoker cooks at 240° F (115° C). Colder outdoor temperatures will lower the cooking heat.

Test your cooker with an oven thermometer. Expect to find that the temperature on the lower shelf will be lower than the upper one, both when testing the cooker and when testing to see if the food is done. Even though the lower shelf is closer to the heat source, heat rises. The upper portion of any enclosed cooking device, from propane barbecue to kitchen oven, is always warmer.

GOOSE PEPPER SAUSAGE

Yield: 4 pounds (2 kg)

I love roast goose, but after you've got one each for Thanksgiving, Christmas, New Year's Eve, Easter, and Mother's Day, you owe it to yourself to try this delicious sausage. It only takes one more goose.

Goose Pepper Sausage

Ingredients
2 large sun-dried tomatoes
⅓ cup (80 ml) boiling water
1 clove garlic
1 medium onion, quartered
1 tablespoon freshly ground black pepper
1 tablespoon crushed red pepper flakes
2 teaspoons salt
3 tablespoons sweet Hungarian paprika
1 tablespoon whole fennel seed
½ teaspoon ground thyme
1 bay leaf, crushed
¼ teaspoon ground coriander
½ cup (125 ml) dry red wine
1 greater Canada goose, boned (about 5¾ pounds/2³⁄₅ kg dressed; 2¾ pounds/1¹⁄₅ kg boned)
1½ pounds (¾ kg) pork butt

Preparation
1. Cover the sun-dried tomatoes with water and soak about 30 minutes, until the tomatoes are soft. Using the coarse plate, grind the goose and pork together into a large bowl and set in the refrigerator.
2. Drain the liquid off the tomatoes and combine them with the garlic, onion, black and red peppers, salt, paprika, fennel, thyme, bay leaf, coriander, and wine in a blender or food processor. Process until the onion is chopped fine but has not turned to liquid. Combine the seasoning mixture with the ground goose and pork. Mix thoroughly, and stuff into hog-sized casings.

Cooking
1. In an electric water smoker: Wipe a small amount of oil on the sausage to prevent it from sticking to the grill. Fill the water pan, and place the sausage on the grill. Cover and plug in the cooker.
2. Cook about 90 minutes, then test the sausage by sticking a meat thermometer into but not through the sausage. Since the sausage contains pork, it should be cooked to 160° F (71° C). Serve hot as a main dish, or refrigerate and use as lunch meat and snacks.

DRY SAUSAGE: HOT AND SLOW SMOKING

VENISON KIELBASA

Yield: 2 pounds (1 kg)

I grew up on Italian sausage and Kosher corned beef. But I didn't know heaven until I stopped in at the Terminal Meat Market in Butte, Montana. Ever since that fateful day, I've been on a pilgrimage to make the perfect wild kielbasa. This quest might not lead to world peace, but with heavenly kielbasa, anything's possible.

Ingredients
1 pound (½ kg) venison
1 pound (½ kg) pork butt
8 cloves garlic, minced
2 teaspoons dried marjoram leaves
2½ teaspoons salt
2 teaspoons sugar
¼ teaspoon cayenne
2 teaspoons black pepper
¾ cup (185 ml) alder chips

Preparation
Grind the meats on the coarse plate of your grinder. In a large bowl, combine the ground meats with the garlic, marjoram, salt, sugar, cayenne, and black pepper. Mix thoroughly by hand and stuff in hog-sized casings to smoke.

Light Smoking in a Kettle Grill
1. For a standard-sized covered kettle grill, open the bottom vent of the barbecue, and start 30 charcoal briquettes. At the same time, place the wood chips in a bowl, cover with water, and allow them to soak.
2. After 25 minutes, when the briquettes are ashen and glowing, place a metal bread pan in the center of the bottom rack, and mound the briquettes on each long side. Drain the wood chips well, and scatter them over and around the briquettes. (Do not pile them on the briquettes or you will douse the coals.)
3. Place the sausages over the bread pan, cover the grill, and open the top vent. Adjust the vents for an optimum smoking temperature of 175°–200° F (80°–93°C). Cook the sausages for approximately 1 hour, till a meat thermometer stuck in the center of the thickest sausage reads 160° F (71° C). The kielbasa can be served hot, as below, or chilled and sliced on crackers. To store, wrap in foil and keep in the refrigerator up to 5 days, or in the freezer up to 4 months.
4. To serve hot and crisp: Add 10–15 cold briquettes to the hot ones halfway through the cooking. By the time the sausages are smoked, the new coals will be ready for a bit of direct-heat grilling. Gently roll the sausages directly over these new coals and cook for 3 minutes a side to get a nice brown finish. Serve in rolls with mustard and a small dollop of prepared, cream-style horseradish.

EXTENDING CHARCOAL LIFE

The cooking life of charcoal briquettes is barely longer than the time it takes to properly and safely smoke these sausages. If you are careful and watch your coals, the above cooking method allows enough time. If you are inclined to handle charcoal briquettes in a leisurely manner, simply add 10–15 cold briquettes among the hot ones just before starting the sausages. The old coals will light the new ones, and will lengthen your cooking time. (For this second fire, use traditional charcoal briquettes, not the self-lighting variety.)

AUGUST ANDOUILLE

Yield: 2 pounds (1 kg)

Andouille is a Cajun-inspired recipe, and while the real stuff is made with only pork, andouille can be adapted into an excellent freezer clearer. Use any white meat—upland bird or rabbit, both legs and breasts—and make it any time of the year. But when hunting season is about to start again, andouille is the answer for those animals that have gravitated to the bottom of the freezer. The best part about andouille is that once it's been smoked you can add it to gumbos, chowders, and jambalaya, as well as venison or fresh bird kabobs, or serve it as an incredibly different wild sausage appetizer.

Ingredients

1½ pounds (¾ kg) various bird and rabbit meat
½ pound (¼ kg) pork butt
3 teaspoons sugar
2 teaspoons salt
¼ teaspoon cayenne pepper
½ teaspoon crushed red pepper flakes
½ teaspoon dried thyme leaves
1 tablespoon hot paprika
¾ cup (185 ml) hickory or alder wood chips

Preparation

1. Grind the wild meat and pork through the coarse plate of your grinder. In a large bowl, combine the sugar, salt, cayenne, red pepper flakes, thyme, and hot paprika, then add the meat and mix thoroughly by hand. Cover and refrigerate for at least 1 hour to let the flavors develop.

2. Test the flavor before stuffing: Fry or microwave a teaspoon-sized chunk of loose sausage, until all the pink is gone. If it is too mild, add red pepper flakes and cayenne equally; too hot, add more wild meat, a quarter pound (⅛ kg) at a time. But be cautious. I've found that spicy sausages always get hotter in the freezer.

3. Stuff in hog-sized casings and smoke.

Cooking

1. For a standard-sized covered kettle grill, open the bottom vent of the barbecue, and start 30 charcoal briquettes. At the same time, place the wood chips in a bowl, cover with water and allow them to soak.

2. After 25 minutes, when the briquettes are ashen and glowing, place a metal bread pan in the center of the bottom rack and mound the briquettes on each long side. Drain the wood chips well, and scatter them over the briquettes. (Do not pile too many in one place or you will cool the fire.)

3. Place the sausages over the bread pan, cover the grill, and open the top vent. Adjust your vents for an optimum smoking temperature of 175°–200° F (78°–93° C). Cook the sausages for approximately 1 hour, till a meat thermometer stuck in the center of the thickest sausage reads 160° F (71° C). The andouille can be served hot, as below, or chilled and sliced on crackers. To store, wrap in foil and keep in the refrigerator up to 5 days, or in the freezer 3–4 months.

4. To serve hot and crisp: Scatter 10–15 cold briquettes amid the hot ones halfway through cooking the sausages. By the time the sausages are smoked, the new coals will be ready for a bit of direct-heat grilling. Gently roll the sausages directly over these new coals, and cook for 3 minutes a side to get a nice brown finish.

Venison Salami

Yield: 5 6-inch (15 cm) salami

Slow smoking the salami allows it to make its own skin, so you don't even need to stuff this sausage into casings. You do, however, need a smoker that will maintain a temperature of 140° F (60° C); barbecues won't do it, nor will a gas or electric water smoker. And while you could make a pale imitation in your kitchen oven, you can't use wood chips indoors. Without your own backyard smoke pit, only an aluminum smoker like the Little Chief will make this deliciously rich, smoky flavor without chasing everyone out of the house. (And only when the ambient air temperature is 50° F/10° C or above.)

Ingredients

2 ½ teaspoons cure (see below)
1 ¼ teaspoons mustard seed
1 ¼ teaspoons pepper, freshly ground
1 teaspoon whole black peppercorns
¾ teaspoon garlic powder
4 tablespoons dry milk powder
½ cup (125 ml) hearty red wine
2 ½ pounds (1 ¼ kg) ground venison
3 cups (750 ml) alder or hickory chips

Preparation

Combine the cure, mustard seed, ground pepper, peppercorns, garlic powder, milk powder, and wine in a large bowl and stir. Once the dry ingredients have dissolved, add the ground venison and mix thoroughly. Cover and refrigerate for 2 days.

Slow Smoking

1. On the third day, soak the wood chips for 30–60 minutes in enough water to cover. While the chips soak, shape the sausage mix into 5 rolls, about 2 inches (5 cm) in diameter. Carefully place the rolls into your Little Chief smoker, so that there's air circulating around all of them. Put 1 cup of the wood chips into the smoker pan, close the smoker up, and turn it on. Three loads of chips (added 1 cup at a time when you see no more smoke) will give you a mild smoke flavor.

2. Smoke 10–12 hours, then check with a meat thermometer inserted in, but not through, a salami on the lowest shelf. (Since this is all venison and no pork, a temperature of 130°–140° F/54°–60° C is sufficient.) Serve sliced with crackers and cheese, or in sandwiches.

Meat Cure Recipe

Yield: 6 teaspoons

You could buy a bag of commercial meat cure at the store, or you can mix up your own. The difference? This cure has no chemicals. With the advent of quality freezers and refrigerators, many home sausage makers have dispensed with the chemicals. It's your choice.

Ingredients

1 teaspoon sugar
5 teaspoons salt

Combine the sugar and salt in a glass jar, cover, and let sit at least 48 hours before using. This gives the cure time to develop flavor, but if you're in a hurry, go ahead and use it immediately. The wait has nothing to do with safety.

Spruce (or Franklin's or Fool's) grouse. (Photograph © William H. Mullins)

INDEX

HELPFUL HINTS

ABOUT THE AUTHOR

For Eileen Clarke, it comes naturally. Her grandfather owned his own butcher shop, her mother was a caterer, and her father loved to eat. Combined with her own love of hunting both big game and birds, it's an invitation to great dining.

Clarke is the author of *The Art of Wild Game Cooking*, a primer for big game, small game, birds, and fish; *The Venison Cookbook*; *The Freshwater Fish Cookbook*, a collection of favorite recipes; and *Classic Freshwater Fish Cooking*, which includes recipes from all over the world and adapts them to today's lifestyle and the North American angler's favorite fish.

Her articles on hunting, conservation, and wild game preparation and cooking techniques have appeared in numerous magazines, including *Field & Stream*, *Bugle*, *Rifle*, *American Hunter*, and *Wyoming Wildlife*. She is also author of a novel, *The Queen of The Legal Tender Saloon*, and is now at work on an all waterfowl cookbook.

In the meantime, she is looking forward to her Lab's second bird season and a snowy fall to make elk hunting just a bit easier than last year.

Photograph © John Barsness